Goethe

Goethe

Peter Boerner

translated by Nancy Boerner

HAUS PUBLISHING • LONDON

First published in Great Britain in 2005 by
Haus Publishing Ltd.
70 Cadogan Place, London SW1X 9AH

This revised edition published in 2013.

Originally published under the title *Johann Wolfgang von Goethe*
by Peter Boerner in the 'rowohlts monographien' series.

A CIP catalogue record for this book is available from the British Library

ISBN 978-1-908323-51-4
eISBN 978-1-908323-52-1

Printed and bound in China by 1010 Printing International Ltd.

Contents

Goethe at the Age of 70. Oil painting by George Dawe.

Goethe on Himself

A portrayal of Goethe that makes use of his own words can draw on an almost endless supply of sources. In addition to his literary, scientific and particularly his autobiographical writings, among them *Poetry and Truth*, the story of his youth, he penned more than 15,000 letters and kept a diary for 52 years. Many visitors, associates and friends recorded their conversations with him. Perhaps not unjustly it has been claimed that there may exist for no other man of letters a similar wealth of documentation.

And yet at times it seems as if we know little more about Goethe than about Dante or Shakespeare. Just as contemporaries felt that his nature could not be described, because he always 'eluded'[1] them, biographers fall silent when faced with the question of his true character. Contributing to this uncertainty are Goethe's writings about himself. In *Poetry and Truth* he only hinted at distressing childhood experiences, and in most of his letters he preferred to talk about external affairs rather than personal matters. Indeed, as he grew older he sought to veil his innermost thoughts behind noncommittal maxims. He wished his literary and autobiographical works to be viewed not as comprehensive confessions in the manner of Rousseau, but more guardedly as *fragments of a great credo*.[2] Werther's fortunes were only one aspect of Goethe's experience; he was never Faust and never Wilhelm Meister. Other than in the spontaneous outpourings of his early letters, he only once openly tried to describe himself. Found among his posthumous papers was a manuscript that probably dates from the summer of 1797, containing what appears to be a draft of a self-portrait:

An always active drive toward literary creativity, which produces both inner and outer consequences, forms the basis of his existence. To prevent this drive from becoming self-consuming he must seek a counterbalance in the real world, for he is not theoretically inclined, but only practical. Hence his ill-advised tendencies: to the fine arts, for which he has no talent; to the world of affairs, for which he has no aptitude; to the sciences, for which he lacks perseverance. But because he approaches all three fields creatively, always aiming to discern the reality of subject and content and to achieve a unity and appropriateness of form, even these mistaken directions of his striving are productive, both outwardly and inwardly . . . In business matters he is competent if there is some substance to them and in the end a lasting result is achieved, or at least something has been accomplished along the way. When obstacles arise, he is not flexible; instead he yields or resists forcibly, perseveres or quits, depending on his convictions or his mood of the moment. He can tolerate whatever results from need, art and craft, yet he must avert his eyes when people act on instinct while pretending to have a purpose. Peculiar to him are a sensitivity and changeability that are influenced by the atmosphere of a present object, causing him either to flee it or to identify with it. This applies to books, to individuals and to groups of people; he cannot read without being animated by the book; even if its tenor is as different as possible from his own, he cannot resist making use of it and trying to produce something similar.[3]

Although Goethe described here more openly than in his subsequent memoirs an inner unrest that constantly drove him, the sketch is significant because it remained a fragment. It almost seems as if he wished to go no further, either for others or for himself. The ultimate comprehension of his identity appeared to him to touch on *those mysteries of life* which, as he noted just a week before his death in a letter to Wilhelm von Humboldt, *there is seldom an hour to ponder.*[4] Despite many insights he gained into the transitions and stages of his growth, the essence of his existence remained for him basically inexpressible. A passage from Job that he cited at the beginning of the essay *Formation and Transformation of Organic Natures* is emblematic of this biography based on his own words:

> *Behold, he passes me*
> *before I perceive him,*
> *and changes*
> *before I notice.*[5]

Childhood and Youth

Johann Wolfgang Goethe, born on 28 August 1749 in the imperial city of Frankfurt am Main, was descended on his father's side from farmers and craftsmen in Thuringia, and on his mother's from a family of scholars and lawyers in southern Germany. After years as a journeyman tailor, his father's father, Friedrich Georg Goethe, settled in Frankfurt, where he married the widow of an innkeeper, thus becoming host of a popular gathering place called 'The Willows'. His son, Johann Caspar Goethe, born in 1710, inherited a considerable fortune. It allowed him to study law and to further his education on tours through France and Italy. After a failed attempt to obtain a post as a municipal administrator, he arranged in 1742 to purchase the title of 'Imperial Councillor', which put him on an equal footing with the town's most distinguished citizens. Without professional responsibilities, from his 32nd year onward he devoted himself to legal studies and his interests in the arts. In 1748 he married Catharina Elisabeth Textor, daughter of the city's Lord Mayor. Of the six children born to the couple, only two survived infancy: Johann Wolfgang and his sister Cornelia, one year his junior.

Goethe's parents' house, sonorously named 'At the Three Lyres', was located only a few hundred paces from the main guardhouse in the centre of town. It typified the life-style of the cultivated citizenry of the time. When Goethe's father remodelled the property, he placed less emphasis on its outward appearance than on *a good and comfortable interior*.[6] He invested much effort in the development of his library and a gallery of paintings.

Souvenirs from his travels adorned the rooms and the spacious second-floor landing. In *Poetry and Truth* Goethe recalled that *a series of Roman scenes*[7] there often drew his gaze. With particular warmth he remembered the view from the third storey of the house: *As I was growing up this was my favourite, not exactly sad, but wistful place to be. Beyond the gardens, beyond the city walls and ramparts one could espy a beautiful fertile plain . . . There I studied my lessons in the summers, waited out thunderstorms and could never see enough of the setting sun. Because I also watched*

Goethe's parental home in Frankfurt. Engraving after a drawing by Friedrich Delkeskamp, 1824. Goethe's father had the original dwelling, consisting of two inadequately connected structures, remodelled to form a splendid home. His son was nine at the time.

the neighbours strolling in their gardens and caring for their flowers, the children playing and groups of people enjoying themselves, I early felt a sense of isolation and a resultant yearning, the influence of which, commensurate with the seriousness and imagination bestowed on me by nature, soon – and subsequently ever more so – became evident.[8]

Goethe accorded his native city much credit for providing the spatial and intellectual environment he enjoyed as a youth. He sketched in his autobiography a picture of the *old commercial town*[9] marked by long-standing traditions, with its streets, alleys, wells, cloisters and churches. Lovingly he described the *beautiful Main River* that *upstream and down drew my gaze,*[10] as well as the pursuits of the residents, their activities and amusements. The boy liked to blend into the crowd around the cathedral or on the 'Römerberg', the square in front of the town hall, which he remembered as a *pleasant place for a stroll*.[11] However, even in his later years he recalled with distaste the *confined, swarming and filthy market place* with its neighbouring *cramped and hideous butcher stalls*.[12] It was here, in a setting unchanged for centuries, that the execution of Susanna Margarethe Brandt, an unwed woman who had killed her newborn child, took place, an event that likely contributed to Goethe's concept of the Gretchen scenes in *Faust*.

It is difficult to gain a comprehensive picture of Goethe's father. In *Poetry and Truth* Goethe refers to him in connection with specific incidents and speaks about his dry, pedantic manner, his strictness toward both himself and others. But he does not give a full characterisation, perhaps because in later years he sensed how much he was becoming like his parent, not only in his appearance, but also in his love of order. Ambiguously, he offered a glimpse of this similarity in a frequently-quoted epigram:

My father gave me my physique
And a serious approach to life.[13]

Goethe's mother. Pastel drawing by Georg Oswald May, 1776.
Goethe included a loving description of his mother in *Poetry and Truth*.
Literary portrayals of her may also be discerned in the characters of Elisabeth in *Götz von Berlichingen* and the mother in *Hermann and Dorothea*.

A counterweight to his father was provided by Goethe's mother, who was *very lively and sunny*.[14] In part because of her age – she was 18 when Goethe was born, while his father was almost 40 – she may have often felt closer to her children than to her husband. Her mediating skills helped prevent severe conflicts between son and father. Goethe later credited his affinity for poetry to her *love of storytelling*.[15] We can only guess how the *happy nature*[16] which he remembered fondly was later tested, for Goethe burnt the letters in which she discussed personal affairs. After her husband's death in 1782, she lived for almost three more decades. Goethe visited his boyhood home only four times after he left it for good in 1775.

Goethe found the closest confidante of his youth in his sister Cornelia. Like her brother, she was *a being neither at peace with herself nor capable of becoming so*,[17] without, however, possessing the gift for literary creativity that enabled him to gain distance from unpleasant experiences. Almost every disagreement caused her prolonged distress. *Only a year younger than I, she had grown with me during my entire conscious life and had thus become bound to me in the innermost way . . . In our early years we played and learnt together, to the point where we could consider ourselves twins, and we retained this affinity, this trust, as our physical and moral capabilities developed. That interest of youth, that amazement at the awakening of sensual feelings which hide behind intellectual conventions, and intellectual needs which take on sensual shapes, all those observations that confuse rather than enlighten, and the resulting aberrations and mistakes, we shared and survived together.*[18]

His father was largely responsible for the rigorous education Goethe received, beginning in early childhood. As was customary among well-to-do families, he was instructed by private tutors, with an emphasis on the liberal arts. Some of the boy's notebooks with Latin and Greek assignments have been preserved and testify to his astonishing mind. The eight-year-old proudly recorded there that he had translated exercises of the public schools' most advanced students. In addition to the classical languages, he

A page from the *Labores Juveniles*, Goethe's exercise book from the years 1757 to 1759.

The text of the 'Colloquium' between P[ater] and F[ilius] = Father and Son, composed in both German and Latin, reads:

P. What are you doing, my son?

F. I'm making a sculpture out of wax.

P. That's what I thought. Oh, when will you finally stop playing with those toys?

F. I'm not playing with toys, but with wax.

P. Simpleton: Can you not know what is meant by toys?

F. Now I remember: but look what a sculptor I have become in a short time.

P. Yes indeed, a wax spoiler.

learnt French, English and Italian, even some Hebrew. When he was ten, he read Aesop, Homer, Virgil and Ovid, as well as the *Thousand and One Nights* and *Robinson Crusoe,* along with folktales about Tyll Owlglass, Doctor Faust and *the whole crew, including the Wandering Jew.*[19]

Goethe's religious upbringing was based in Lutheranism, the predominant creed in Frankfurt. Attendance at church services was complemented by readings at home of the Holy Scriptures, both the Old and New Testaments. Although he later distanced himself from ecclesiastical forms of Christianity, Goethe acknowledged that he owed a large part of his education to the Bible. His father's conservative stance in religious matters can be recognised in his rejection of Klopstock's *Messiah.* Goethe and his sister were deeply impressed by the book, which they read secretly.

Of significance for the boy's intellectual development was the Lisbon earthquake of 1 November 1755, one of the greatest catastrophes of the time. Although in writing *Poetry and Truth* Goethe tried to play down disturbing experiences, he did not conceal there that the event severely shook his peace of mind: *More quickly than the news itself, the aftershocks spread throughout a wide area; weaker tremors were felt in numerous locations; many springs fell still. All the greater was the effect of the news itself, which travelled rapidly, first with general information and then with all the terrible details. Afterwards, the pious did not stint on severe reprimands to their congregations . . . The boy, who absorbed all this, experienced no little bewilderment. God, the Creator and Sustainer of heaven and earth, whom the First Article of Faith had portrayed as so wise and merciful, had allowed the just to suffer the same fate as the unjust, thus in no way proving to be fatherly. In vain the young mind sought to come to grips with such observations, but this was all the less possible because even sages and scholars could not agree on how to interpret the phenomenon.*[20]

Goethe's father in 1774. Watercolour by Georg Friedrich Schmoll. To Chancellor von Müller, Goethe remarked in 1830: *My father was a fine person, although he lacked a certain agility and flexibility. He was old-fashioned with regard to religion, but he did not object to my speculations and opinions, even taking pleasure in the fact that his son was an odd chap.*

Other events had a lasting impact on Goethe, as well. When the Seven Years War between Prussia and Austria broke out in 1756, the former led by Frederick the Second, the latter by Maria Theresa, and the world was *called upon not only to observe but to judge,*[21] he became aware how political affairs could affect his own life: *Just as in my sixth year the Lisbon earthquake had caused me to regard God's goodness with some suspicion, now, because of Frederick, I came to doubt the objectivity of the public . . . The most obvious achievements were scorned and ridiculed; the most illustrious deeds, if not repudiated, at the least were played down; and such unjustice was done to the one man who was obviously superior to all his contemporaries. This was the work not of a mob, but of outstanding men, among whom I counted my grandfather and uncles.*[22]

The differences of opinion between his grandfather Textor, who favoured Austria, and his father, who was inclined toward Prussia, led to tensions and finally to an open breach within the family. Without understanding the political issues, but drawn by Frederick's personality, Goethe sided with his father. *And so I, too, was Prussian-oriented – or, more correctly, Fritz-oriented – for what did Prussia mean to us?*[23]

Frankfurt was directly affected by the war when the French, Austria's allies, attacked in January 1759 and subsequently occupied the city. The lower floors of the Goethes' house were requisitioned as quarters for the leading official of the French administration, Royal Lieutenant Count François de Thoranc. Although Thoranc disagreed with his landlord on a variety of issues, he treated the son of the house with fatherly affection. As an adult, Goethe thanked him with an appreciative portrayal in *Poetry and Truth*. He mentioned in particular the Count's love of art and his commissioning of works by local painters, among them Johann Konrad Seekatz. As most of the pictures were executed in his parents' house, the boy became acquainted with the milieu of the visual arts.

A novelty of the occupation was the presence of a French repertory company, whose performances Goethe was permitted to attend. As an 11-year-old he viewed plays by Racine and Molière, and came into contact with the world of the actors, as well. His growing interest in the stage, stimulated earlier by a puppet theatre, is recalled in some scenes of his novel *Wilhelm Meister's Theatrical Calling*.

It was during the occupation of Frankfurt that Goethe produced his first poems. The closing lines of a rhymed New Year's greeting, offered in 1757 to his maternal grandparents, were beginning to be fulfilled:

> *These are early efforts for reflection;*
> *Soon my pen will show perfection.*[24]

With increasing ease the youth composed a variety of lyrics, some in competition with friends. On his 13th birthday he presented his father with a quarto volume of verses. Few of these pieces have been preserved. Spared were only parts of *Poetic Thoughts on Christ's Descent into Hell* and fragments of a drama dealing with the fall of Belshazzar, the Babylonian king whom God punished for his blasphemy.

It was because of his talent that Goethe became involved in a painful contretemps, when a group of young people induced him to compose fictitious letters and then used them without his knowledge for deceptive purposes. The 14-year-old was attracted to a girl in this group, identified as Gretchen in *Poetry and Truth*. But when she testified at a formal investigation of the affair that she had never taken him seriously, he distanced himself: *I found it intolerable that a girl at most a couple of years older than I should have considered me a child, when I thought myself to be a clever and adroit chap.*[25] In his reminiscences the background for this episode, artfully combining experience and fiction, is formed by the coronation in April 1764 of Joseph II as Holy Roman Emperor. Goethe's descriptions bring to life the colourful spectacle of this *political-religious ceremony.*[26]

Student Years

At 16, Goethe was ready to attend university. Had he been permitted to follow his own inclinations, he would have taken up classical studies at Göttingen, but his father insisted on the university at Leipzig, which he himself had attended. He assumed that his son would become versed in jurisprudence, receive his doctorate at Leipzig or a second institution and then pursue a career in administrative law.

Feeling like *a prisoner who has cast off his chains,*[27] and provided with a generous line of credit, Goethe arrived in Leipzig on 3 October 1765. Known for its trade fairs, and shaped by *a recent period of commerce, wealth and opulence,*[28] the city was suffused with the spirit of the Rococo. It impressed the youth who had grown up within the confines of a more traditional environment. He gave himself up to the new influences, transforming himself into an aesthete, who cut a *fine figure.*[29]

His early enthusiasm, however, was followed by disappointments. Neither the classes in law nor in the humanities held his interest. Gellert, the poet, whose

Goethe in 1765. Oil painting by Anton Johann Kern. The 15-year-old Kern portrayed his 16-year-old friend shortly before he left Frankfurt to study at Leipzig.

lectures on German letters he had been eager to attend, lost the student's respect because in long-winded perorations he dismissed the rising stars of the day, such as Klopstock, Wieland and Lessing. Another teacher, Gottsched, once considered the land's leading author, had become an object of ridicule due to his immoderate vanity. On top of all this, Goethe discovered that his new acquaintances neither appreciated his lyrics nor – in anti-Prussian Saxony – shared his partisanship for King Frederick. In a letter to a friend in Frankfurt, he described his disillusionment by picturing himself as a worm that aspires to higher things:

> *I saw that my majestic flight*
> *(As it seemed to me) was nothing but an*
> *Attempt of a worm in the dust, which sees the eagle*
> *Soaring to the sun and thus*
> *Yearns to do the same. It struggles upward, squirms,*
> *And timidly strains every nerve,*
> *But stays in the dust. And then a wind arises quickly,*
> *Raises the dust in eddies, and also lifts the worm.*
> *It feels mighty, like an eagle, and rejoices*
> *In the giddiness. But suddenly the wind abates.*
> *The dust sinks downward,*
> *And with it the worm. Now it creeps along just as before.*[30]

He found counsel in Ernst Wolfgang Behrisch, the tutor of a young count. Goethe would later call him one of the *queerest fish in the world*,[31] but he understood how *to tame my restlessness and impatience*.[32] With his sure sense of good taste, Behrisch became the first critical reader of Goethe's poetry. Only a few of the verses, composed in the light 'Anacreontic' style of the time, met with Behrisch's approval, but those he copied in an elegant hand and assembled into a book, *Annette*, that has been preserved. Aside from Behrisch, two artists, Johann Michael Stock and Adam

Friedrich Oeser, were helpful to Goethe. He took instruction in etching and engraving from Stock, and studied drawing with Oeser. A friend of Winckelmann, the renowned art historian, Oeser acquainted Goethe with the precepts of classicism and attempted to dissuade him from his predilection for the *curlicued, shell-adorned nature*[33] of the Rococo.

Leipzig brought the 17-year-old the first real passion of his life. In the tavern of the Schönkopf family, where he took his meals, he met the owners' daughter, Anna Katharina, called Käthchen, *a pretty and good-natured girl*,[34] and became enamoured of her with all the vehemence of his temperament. However, his *unfounded and petty jealousies*[35] strained the relationship, which ended in a friendly parting. In his first completed drama, *The Lover's Caprices*, a reflection of pastoral plays popular at the time, Goethe depicted the stress generated by his feelings. Later, in *Poetry and Truth*, he indicated that as early as during his Leipzig stay he had experienced a need to free himself from troubling

The Promenade in Leipzig. Coloured engraving after a drawing by Johann August Rosmäsler, 1777. Because of its elegance, Leipzig was called *Little Paris*. The Promenade between the Thomas and the Franciscan gates was a favourite meeting place for young men and women.

emotions by putting them into words: *And so began that inclination from which I was unable to deviate throughout my entire life, namely to turn whatever delighted, distressed or otherwise preoccupied me into a picture, a poem. In that way I came to terms with it, both in order to clarify my conceptions of external things and to attain an inner peace. No one could have needed this talent more than I, whose nature cast him constantly from one extreme to another. Thus all the things that I have voiced are simply fragments of a great credo, which this volume [Poetry and Truth] will make a valiant attempt to synthesize.*[36]

After three years at Leipzig, Goethe experienced a crisis. His constant round of amusements and studies resulted in considerable strain, and culminated in a physical collapse. Stricken with a haemorrhage in July 1768, he drifted for several days *between life and death*.[37] *Like a shipwreck survivor*,[38] he returned to Frankfurt. It took almost a year and a half for him to recover fully and lose the fear that he might have consumption. Under the guidance of Susanna von Klettenberg, an adherent of the Moravian Brethren and a friend of his mother, he began during his convalescence to read mystical and pietistic publications, among them Gottfried Arnold's *History of the Church and Its Heretics*.

The personality of his mentor deeply impressed Goethe. Her encouragement helped him to overcome the disquiet he had experienced in Leipzig: *She had her own interpretation of my restlessness, my impatience, my striving, my searching, investigating, brooding and wavering: she made no secret of her conviction that all this came from my not having reconciled myself with God. Now I had believed since childhood that I stood quite well with Him; indeed, I imagined after a number of experiences that He might even owe me something, and I was brazen enough to believe that there were even a few things for which I should forgive Him. This notion arose from my boundless goodwill, to which, it seemed to me, He could have offered more help. One can imagine how often my friend and I came to blows over this, but always in the most amicable fashion, frequently ending in the conclusion that I was a silly fellow who sometimes had to be indulged.*[39]

In addition to Susanna von Klettenberg, a doctor named Johann Metz, who seems to have been knowledgeable about homeopathic principles, contributed to both the physical and the mental well-being of the convalescent. Under his direction Goethe immersed himself in the writings of Paracelsus, as well as in Georg von Welling's *Opus magocabbalisticum et theosophicum*, and even conducted alchemistic experiments. His interest in observing natural processes was awakened. Characteristic of his thought is a letter he sent in February 1769 to Friederike Oeser, the daughter of his Leipzig drawing teacher: *My life is currently devoted to philosophy. Shut in, alone, a compass, paper, pen and ink and two books my only equipment. And in this simple way I often come so close to realising the truth, closer than others with their bookish learning. A great scholar is seldom a great philosopher. Those who have pored laboriously through many volumes are prone to scorn the light and simple book of nature, but there is nothing true that is not simple.*[40]

Strasbourg Cathedral. Engraving from Goethe's collection. Goethe assumed the cathedral to be a work of German architecture because Alsace and Strasbourg had previously belonged to Germany. Use of the term 'Gothic' to describe European structures of the 12th to 16th centuries became common only with the later study of the history of architecture.

Around Easter 1770, Goethe left home again, this time to complete his studies in Strasbourg, which was largely German-speaking, although it belonged politically to France. More than any other period of his life, the year and a half that Goethe spent there brought him a new beginning in everything he experienced and wrote. On his arrival, he was overcome by the sight of Strasbourg's cathedral. Unlike most of his contemporaries, the 20-year-old appreciated the grandeur of the Gothic edifice, which at the time was considered ostentatious. In the tribute *On German Architecture*, written two years later, he was able to recall the feeling it aroused in him: *What an unexpected sensation surprised me as I approached the sight! My soul was filled with a tremendous, indelible impression, which I could savour and enjoy, but in no way understand or explain, because it was made up of a thousand harmonising details . . . How often in the twilight was my eye, weary from inquiring scrutiny, refreshed by the friendly peace when the countless parts melted into one expanse, which now stood, simple and grand, before my soul, making possible the blissful evolution of my ability to enjoy and to understand. Becoming evident to me, in faint intimations, was the genius of a great master craftsman.*[41]

After an initial exploration of *lovely Alsace*,[42] Goethe's life in Strasbourg was defined by intense study. Instead of concentrating on jurisprudence, however, to which no *inner compulsion drove*[43] him, he attended lectures on medicine and political theory. He also delved into historical, philosophical and theological questions. In a notebook he listed the authors he read or intended to read, ranging from Socrates and Plato through Thomas à Kempis to Rousseau and Moses Mendelssohn. To a Frankfurt acquaintance who had asked for advice about planning his studies, he wrote: *When you enter academic life, the first thing you will find are a hundred people like me. 'He wasn't the only one!' you will think, and then you will go further and find a hundred better than I. You will measure me against this new standard, find all kinds of shortcomings, and then I am lost. It is difficult to judge fairly someone one has considered perfect but then finds to be defective in even one area . . . To devote oneself to subjects to which the intellect is inclined, to compare things, put everything in its place, assess every value, that is what we have to do now. In pursuing this we should be nothing but should want to become everything, and in particular should not stop and rest more often than dictated by the demands of a weary mind and body.*[44]

What Goethe recommended in this letter he required of himself, as well. Indeed, the exhortation to self-education, *we should be nothing but should want to become everything* – which he also articulated later, including in *Faust* and *Wilhelm Meister*, and which he repeated almost verbatim to his associate von Müller in 1830: *One must constantly change, renew, rejuvenate oneself in order not to stagnate*[45] – led him in Strasbourg to extreme efforts: to overcome spells of dizziness that ocasionally afflicted him, he made a habit of climbing to the top of the cathedral tower; he learnt to endure loud noise, which he detested, by following the drummers at military exercises; and in anatomy classes he tried to accustom himself to the *most disgusting sights,*[46] despite an innate revulsion.

Just as he had done in Leipzig, Goethe made close friends in Strasbourg. He frequently took his meals with the physician Jung-Stilling, a pietist, and the poet Jakob Lenz. Most consequential was an encounter with Johann Gottfried Herder, who was spending some time in Strasbourg due to the need for an eye operation. Much later, long after his break with the splenetic old man that Herder became, Goethe described their first acquaintanceship, grateful for the encouragement he had received: *The influence of this good-humoured blusterer was considerable and significant. He was five years older than I, which in youth makes a great difference; and because I recognised him for what he was, because I tried to appreciate what he had already achieved, he was able to attain immense influence over me . . . His conversations were always substantive, whether he was posing questions, giving answers or communicating in some other way. Daily, even hourly, he impelled me to new views.*[47]

Under Herder's guidance, Goethe finally broke with everything Rococo. Herder led him to the anti-rationalist, *sibylline*[48] ideas of Johann Georg Hamann; filled him with enthusiasm for the depth of Shakespeare; drew his attention to Macpherson's

Ossianic creations; and introduced him to folk poetry, which he recognised as *the oldest documentation*[49] of literary expression. *I got to know poetry from a completely new perspective, in another sense than before, and one that greatly appealed to me.*[50] Inspired by Herder, he became convinced that it is more relevant for writers, and for artists as well, to let themselves be led by their emotions than to put their faith in acquired skills. He adhered to this premise throughout his life.

The parsonage in Sesenheim, with a barn and draw-well. Red chalk drawing by Goethe, 1771.

The counterbalance to such intellectual activities was a new love. A month after meeting Herder, Goethe was introduced to the family of Johann Jakob Brion, pastor in Sesenheim, a village a few hours from Strasbourg. The story of his first ride there from the city, his memory of being greeted by the hospitable clergyman and his description of the cleric's two daughters are among the most lyrical parts of *Poetry and Truth*. The younger of the two sisters, Friederike, appeared to the visitor to be *truly a most lovely star in this rural heaven.*[51] After their first meeting, Goethe wrote to her from Strasbourg. A draft of this letter of 15 October 1770 is the only record preserved from their relationship: *Dear new friend, I don't hesitate to address you thus, for even if otherwise I understand only little of the language of the eyes, at our first glance my eye found in yours a hope of this friendship, and I could swear our hearts felt the same. As affectionate and good as I know you to be, should you not be kindly disposed toward me, when I am so fond of you? . . . To be sure, Mademoiselle, Strasbourg never seemed so empty to me as now. I hope it will improve, when time has dimmed the memory of our droll and playful merry-making. But am I able or willing to forget that? No, I would rather keep the slight heartache, and write to you often.*[52]

The break with literary conventions that occurred under Herder's influence and the attraction to Friederike Brion were forces that triggered in Goethe a flood of lyrics, more emotional than almost any yet known in German letters. A ride, begun late in the day as a *passionate undertaking*,[53] brought him to Sesenheim by the light of the moon and inspired the poem *Welcome and Farewell*. Another creation was the *May Song*, with the opening line *How dazzlingly beautiful is Nature*. In the tone of folk songs that at Herder's urging he had *plucked from the throats of the oldest grannies*,[54] he wrote *Rose on the Heath*.

Nonetheless, after only a few months, traces of doubt tinged the idyllic mood. More clearly than in the sublimated reminiscence in *Poetry and Truth*, this is evident in a letter Goethe sent from Sesenheim in early summer 1771 to one of his Strasbourg dining companions: *The state of my heart is peculiar. The most pleasing countryside, people who love me, a round of joys! 'Are not all your childhood dreams fulfilled?' I sometimes ask myself, when feasting my eyes on this horizon of bliss; 'are these not the fairy gardens for which you yearned?' – They are, they are! I feel it, dear friend, and feel that one is not an iota happier when one attains what one has craved. The counterweight! the counterweight! that fate casts into every bliss! Dear friend, one needs much courage not to become discontented in this world. As a boy, I playfully planted a little cherry tree; it grew, and I had the joy of seeing it bloom. A May frost spoiled my pleasure in the blossoms, and I had to wait a year for beautiful, ripe cherries; but the birds ate most of them before I could try even one; another year it was the caterpillars, then a nibbling neighbour, then mould; and yet, when I am the master of a garden, I shall plant cherry trees again. Despite all the mishaps, there is still so much fruit that one can eat one's fill.*[55]

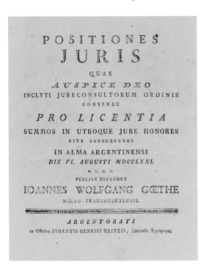

Positiones Juris. Title page of the 56 theses that Goethe defended to attain the title of Licentiate of Law, printed in Strasbourg in 1771. In Germany a licentiate degree was regarded as equivalent to a doctorate. Goethe was thus entitled to call himself 'Doctor juris'.

Goethe's attempt to complete his studies by attaining a doctorate in jurisprudence failed. The dissertation he submitted, on a theme of ecclesiastical history – *the legislator is not only authorised but obligated to establish a certain community of values from which neither the clergy nor the laity may exempt themselves*[56] – was rejected. Views advanced in it, such as the notion that Christian teachings did not come directly from Jesus but were proclaimed by others under his name, unnerved the faculty. As a substitute for a doctorate, Goethe was permitted to apply for the degree of licentiate of law, a simpler process that involved publicly defending a set of theses. The issues he chose to address, selected with the help of a tutor, ranged from natural law to inheritance law to criminal trial procedure. It is doubtful, however, whether he was serious about the examination. His friends appeared to interpret some of his theses as bromides or even gibes at his teachers. The disputation, held in Latin, took place on 6 August 1771, *under challenges from my table mates, with much jollity, indeed flippancy.*[57]

Two days after the defence, Goethe visited Friederike Brion for the last time, without letting her know that he would not return. Only after he was back in Frankfurt did he sever the connection, recognising the action was due to his own uncertainty. In his memoirs he acknowledged later: *Friederike's response to a written farewell rent my heart . . . Now I truly felt the loss that she suffered, and I saw no possibility to counter it or even to soften it. She was always on my mind; I missed her constantly, and the worst was that I could not forgive myself my own misery. I was guilty here for the first time; I had deeply wounded the finest heart, and so this period of gloomy repentance was hugely painful, indeed unbearable.*[58]

Storm and Stress

Upon his return from Strasbourg, at the age of 22, Goethe was admitted to practise as an attorney at Frankfurt's municipal court. He did not, however, fulfill his father's expectation that he would achieve a respectable career. During the next four years he participated in only 28 lawsuits: he had other things in mind than leading a bourgeois life. There was no trace of the obsessiveness with which he would devote himself to legal matters only a few years later in Weimar.

Goethe's literary productions at the time still reflected his Strasbourg experiences. He translated Macpherson's sombre *Songs of Selma*, later incorporated into his *Sorrows of Young Werther*. By immersing himself in Shakespeare's plays he tried to *prepare himself for a more open philosophy and intellectual delights as lyrical as they are true.*[59] This effort gave impetus to his first preserved prose text, the essay *On Shakespeare's Day*. In it he not only professed his admiration for the author of *Hamlet*, who at that time was not well known in Germany, but he formulated the agenda of the *literary revolution*[60] that would come to be known as 'Storm and Stress' (Sturm und Drang). He read into Shakespeare the objectives that he and his contemporaries would propound: a departure from rule-bound French drama and its German imitators, and the supremacy of the natural in both life and literature. To have *marrow in one's bones*[61] was the challenge for the individual. And the motto for the new directions, resounding again and again, was 'Nature'. 'Nature' signified the entirety of human character as well as the totality of the universe, but it also stood for abolition of the dualistic concepts of good and evil, and the recognition that human beings are destined to perish. Or, as Goethe found in Shakespeare: *His pieces all revolve around the mysterious point that no philosopher has yet discerned and defined, in which that unique aspect of our being, the imagined freedom of will, collides with the necessary course of the cosmos.*[62]

To better apprehend the conflict between the individual and the *necessary course of the cosmos*, Goethe turned to drama. He became fascinated by the *heroic spirit*[63] of Socrates, and then by a contemporary of Luther, Götz von Berlichingen, a Franconian knight whose autobiography he had read in Strasbourg: *My whole creative drive is devoted to an enterprise that has caused me to forget Homer and Shakespeare and everything else. I am dramatizing the story of one of the noblest Germans, rescuing the memory of an upright man, and all the work that it has cost me has been pure enjoyment.*[64]

By marshalling all the strength of which he felt capable and *casting it at the project to come to grips with it and impel it forward*,[65] Goethe completed a first version of *Götz von Berlichingen* in just

Goethe's study in his parents' house in Frankfurt. The pencil drawing washed with ink and watercolour is thought to be a self-portrait, executed after 1770. The three-cornered hat and the sword on the wall are indicative of Goethe's walking tours on the outskirts of the city, while the easel points to his artistic interests.

over six weeks, toward the end of 1771. In the person of Götz he created a Storm and Stress protagonist: an independent knight who courageously challenges the authorities of his era. The piece,

Whom you do not abandon, Genius,
Neither rain nor storm
Causes his heart to shudder.
Whom you do not abandon, Genius,
In the face of rain clouds,
In the face of hailstorms,
Will sing
Like the lark,
Up above.

Wanderer's Storm Song, first stanza

which has 59 scene changes and no continuity of either time or place, represented Goethe's irrevocable break with traditional drama.

Goethe's attitude reflected his contemporaries' glorification of a new life-style. He paid little attention to his parents' customs; as an attorney he had to accept the court's rebuke for his 'unseemly manner of writing';[66] he made fun in farces and parodies of celebrities and even of his own friends; dabbled in alchemistic experiments; and sought company among people with similar inclinations, in Frankfurt and in neighbouring towns, including Darmstadt: *I became accustomed to living on the road, travelling back and forth like a courier between the mountains and the plain. Often, alone or in company, I walked through my home city as if it meant nothing to me . . . More than ever I was focused on the open world and untrammelled nature. En route I sang to myself, strange hymns and dithyrambs, of which one, entitled Wanderer's Storm Song, survives. I sang this half-nonsense with passion, trying to drown out terrible storms along the way.*[67]

In Darmstadt Goethe became involved with a group that championed the culture of sensibility. Calling themselves the 'Society of Saints', they included Herder's fiancée, Caroline Flachsland, and Johann Heinrich Merck, an official in the Hessian government. Merck, roguish and *whimsical*, yet *gifted with sure and incisive judgement*,[68] took over the role of Goethe's critical mentor earlier filled by Herder. Goethe contributed a number of articles to a review Merck edited, the *Frankfurter Gelehrte Anzeigen*.

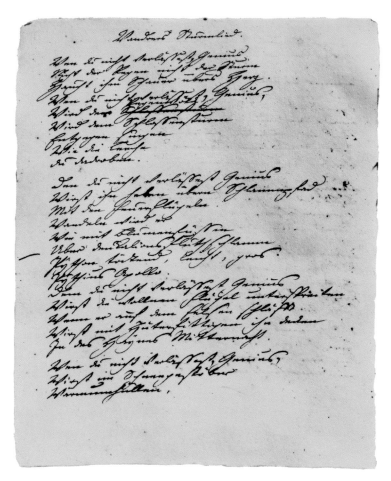

Goethe's manuscript of the *Wanderer's Storm Song*, composed in April 1772.

On his father's advice, in May 1772 Goethe volunteered as an intern at the Imperial Supreme Court in Wetzlar, north of Frankfurt. He felt that the change of location would give him an opportunity to follow his inclinations more than he could at home. In a letter to Herder he described his current preoccupation: *Since the last time I heard from you, the Greeks have become my only concern. First I limited myself to Homer; then, in order to understand Socrates, I took up Xenophon and Plato. Eventually something drew me to Pindar, where I am still. In addition, a good spirit finally has clarified for me why I have an unruly nature. It came to me when I was reading Pindar's words* επικρατειν δυνασθαι *[to be able to take control]. If you stand boldly in a chariot, with four fresh horses straining wildly at the reins, you steer their power with your whip, urging the straying to go forward, the rearing to calm down, and you drive and steer, change direction, whip, stop and then drive them onwards again, until all sixteen legs fall into step and carry you to your goal – that is mastery, virtuosity.*[69]

The impression made by the 23-year-old was captured in a letter by one of his Wetzlar associates: 'He has many talents, is a true genius and a man of character; possesses an extraordinary imagination and hence expresses himself mainly in images and parables . . . His way of thinking is noble, free of preconceptions; he acts as he likes, without bothering to consider whether it is pleasing to others. His convictions are not yet solidly grounded, and he is still striving to find a systematic philosophy. He has a high regard for Rousseau, but does not blindly revere him . . . He hates scepticism, strives for truth and for an understanding of certain central issues, although he feels he already comprehends the most important ones; as far as I can tell, he does not as yet. He strives for truth, but places more importance on the feeling of truth than on its demonstration.'[70]

Goethe became close friends with the author of this sketch, Johann Christian Kestner, a lawyer from Bremen, and with his fiancée, Charlotte Buff, called Lotte. Despite their fondness for each other, tensions arose when Goethe's feelings for Lotte grew passionate. Following Merck's advice, he decided – after less than four months in Wetzlar – *to leave voluntarily*, before he *might be driven away by the unbearable state of affairs*.[71] He returned to Frankfurt after a brief stay in Ehrenbreitstein, where he met with

Merck, as well as with the author Sophie von La Roche and her daughter Maximiliane, whom he found charming.

At home, his still painful memories of Lotte Buff were joined by new tensions arising from changes in the once-familiar environment. His sister married one of his friends, attorney Johann Georg Schlosser, and moved with him to Emmendingen in Baden, in southwestern Germany. Maximiliane von La Roche took up residence in Frankfurt as the wife of Peter Brentano, a merchant, but a congenial relationship did not develop due to her husband's jealousy. Lotte Buff and Kestner were married in 1773, without, as they had promised, informing Goethe. On top of this melancholy state of affairs came the news that a distant acquaintance from Wetzlar, named Jerusalem, had taken his own life because of his desperate love for the wife of a friend. That was the catalyst for the conception of *The Sorrows of Young Werther* around the beginning of 1774: *Jerusalem's death shook me out of a dream. Because I could not just passively observe what he and I had experienced, as my similar circumstances aroused in me a passionate need for action, it was inevitable that I should pour into the*

Charlotte Buff as a 17-year-old, ink silhouette. Goethe received the portrait in October 1772, about a month after he left Wetzlar without taking leave of Lotte and Kestner. A note attached to it, 'Lotte, good night', has been dated to 17 July 1774. At that time Lotte and Kestner had been married for almost a year, and Goethe had completed *The Sorrows of Young Werther*. In 1816, Lotte, as wife of then Privy Councillor Kestner, came from Hanover to Weimar to visit relatives, and also met with Goethe. Thomas Mann gave literary form to this encounter in his novel *Lotte in Weimar*.

work all the ardour that does not allow any distinction between the literary and the real. I completely isolated myself, even forbade visits by my friends, and I put aside everything internal that did not pertain to this particular situation . . . Under these circumstances I wrote Werther in four weeks, without previously having put to paper an outline of the whole or a draft of any part of it.[72]

Autumn 1774 brought the publication of *The Sorrows of Young Werther*, in the form of an epistolary novel. Its reception by the reading public was unique in the history of German letters. Shortly after the 200-page volume appeared, it sold out. Reprints followed, then pirated editions. Young people devoured it with tears in their eyes. Some dressed like the novel's protagonists, Werther and Lotte. In Germany it was for a time the best-known book after the Bible. Cases of suicide were associated with it. There was talk of a 'Werther fever'.

What accounted for the powerful effect of this story about a young man who was, as Goethe wrote in a letter, *endowed with deep and pure sensitivity and true acuity, but who lost himself in crazy dreams, undermined himself with risky uncertainties, until finally, deranged by unhappy passions and especially an unrequited love, put a bullet through his head?*[73]

Goethe's explanation for the phenomenon included the widespread tendency toward sentimental feeling in the third quarter of the 18th century; influences from English literature, including Young's melancholy *Night Thoughts* and Sterne's *Sentimental Journey*; and also, not least, Rousseau's worship of nature – in short, the mood of a generation that, *suffering from unfulfilled passions, with no external impetus to pursue significant activities, and with no prospect other than to persevere in a dull, plodding, bourgeois existence*, was open to a *sick, youthful madness.*[74] Suicide, until then considered an offence, was justified by Werther as a *illness unto death*[75] – a term later taken up by Kierkegaard – and drew understanding, even sympathy. Criticism of social conditions, as well as

Werther's negative attitude toward a career, furthered the mood of Weltschmerz. And yet the book, which almost contrary to Goethe's intent became a symbol of protest against the ruling authorities, signified more than just a contemporary event. As in *Götz von Berlichingen*, the conflict between the individual and the *necessary course of the cosmos*[76] – first defined in the Shakespeare essay – manifested itself: the incompatibility between the soulful human being and the real world leads to Werther's downfall. Without being guilty, he is crushed by the excess of his own feelings, and thus by his very nature.

The elements of protest contained in *The Sorrows of Young Werther* prompted critical responses. Members of the enlightened bourgeoisie, the clergy and conservative governments recognised the book's anarchic tendencies. Some saw in the figure of Werther an outsider, a deranged person whose attitude represented a threat to the established order. There were repudiations and rejoinders. Seen as an apologia for suicide, the work was banned in some cities, including Leipzig, centre of the German book trade. Its impact was further apparent in a series of parodies, among them Friedrich Nicolai's *Sorrows and Joys of Werther, the Man*. Goethe replied to it with the almost obscene satire *Nicolai at Werther's Grave*.

Goethe at the age of 24. Miniature in oil by the Frankfurt painter Johann Daniel Bager. The picture was commissioned by Johann Kaspar Lavater for inclusion in his *Physiognomical Fragments*. At Lavater's suggestion, Goethe sat for the artist with smoothly combed and powdered hair.

As a result of all these reactions, both positive and negative, at the age of only 25 Goethe had become one of the best-known authors in Germany.

Many contemporaries sang his praises. Gottfried August Bürger, already famous as the author of the ballad *Lenore,* established contact, as did the brothers Christian and Friedrich Leopold zu Stolberg. Klopstock paid him a visit in Frankfurt, and even believed he had found a disciple. Johann Kaspar Lavater, the Zürich clergyman, proponent of an exaggerated cult of sensibility, sought his friendship. With Lavater and Johann Bernhard Basedow, a champion of educational reform, Goethe took a trip on the Lahn and Rhine rivers in the summer of 1774. In Düsseldorf he was fêted by Friedrich Heinrich Jacobi: 'Goethe is a genius from head to toe; an obsessive, I might add, who can almost never act without purpose.'[77]

While young writers, to some extent under the influence of *Werther,* were immersing themselves in a mood of Weltschmerz, Goethe himself was already on the way to distancing himself from it, mostly by means of an increased productivity. Nearly no other period of his life saw as many plans and drafts as his last years in Frankfurt. He admitted at the time, *if I did not write dramas, I would perish,*[78] and almost all his internal and external experiences were converted into literary form. *My creative talent . . . did not abandon me for even a moment; what I experienced during my waking daytime hours often reshaped itself at night in regular dreams, and when I opened my eyes there appeared to me either a singular new creation or another portion of an existing one. Usually I wrote everything down by earliest daylight; but in the evening, too, even deep into the night, after wine and company had elevated my spirits, one could demand of me what one wished; all I needed was an opportunity that showed some substance, and then I was eager and ready to work.*[79]

Some pieces that Goethe conceived between 1773 and 1775 flowed into his emotive letters. Others became odes, songs or dramatic sketches with a considerable variety of content. How many drafts were lost, is unknown. He consigned to flames various manuscripts on which he had worked, including parts of a tragedy about Caesar. One of his most ambitious projects, a drama *Prometheus*, of which his defiant ode *Protect Your Heaven, Zeus* is reminiscent, remained a fragment. A series of scenes for a *Faust* tragedy was sketched out, but did not progress. Completed were only a few short plays, among them *Concerto dramatico* and *Fair in Plundersweilern*; the farce *Gods, Heroes and Wieland*; and two singspiels, *Erwin and Elmire* and *Claudine of Villa Bella*.

In the years before and after the publication of *Werther*, Goethe also tried to clarify religious issues for himself. Reflective of this pursuit is a pamphlet that appeared anonymously, as was the custom at the time: the *Letter of the Pastor in *** to the New Pastor in ****. Under the guise of a rural Lutheran clergyman, Goethe expressed his thoughts on various theological trends. He rejected dogmatism, orthodoxy and rationalism; supported a Christianity of pietistic inclination; and also, six years before Lessing's *Nathan the Wise*, advocated tolerance without indifference. Content and format of the tract pointed to the influence of Rousseau, Hamann and Herder. And by having his pastor state, *There was never a real Church on earth*,[80] Goethe revived a theme from Gottfried Arnold's *History of the Church and Its Heretics*, known to him through Susanna von Klettenberg, that Christian doctrine was truly pure only in the first century, and thereafter became removed from the intentions of its creator. How far Goethe was prepared to go is only hinted at in the *Letter of the Pastor*. More is revealed in the epic poem *The Eternal Jew*, written in 1774, but not published until after his death: instead of presenting an idealised view of a spiritual community, he here subjected clerical institutions to sarcastic criticism.

Goethe's last year in Frankfurt, 1775, brought him a new love. With Lili Schönemann, the 16-year-old daughter of a Frankfurt merchant, he experienced one of the *happiest*[81] times of his life. The relationship progressed to a formal engagement, but their different life styles and faiths (Lili's family belonged to the Reformed

Elisabeth von Türckheim, née Schönemann, Goethe's Lili, at the age of 24. Pastel portrait by Franz Bernhard Frey. Three years after Goethe ended his engagement with Lili, she married the Strasbourg banker Bernhard von Türckheim. Goethe visited the couple in 1779 on his way to Switzerland.

Church), as well as a lack of understanding between their parents, resulted in tensions. Goethe wavered between his attraction to Lili and the fear that he might become dissatisfied with a life of *domestic bliss*.[82] In letters sent in February 1775 to the younger sister of the two Counts Stolberg, Auguste, who had initiated an enthusiastic correspondence with him after the appearance of *Werther*, he described to his *dear friend, well known to my heart but never seen by my eyes*,[83] the picture of a *double life*: *If, my dear, you can imagine a Goethe in a coat with braided trim, illumined by the meaningless brilliance of wall sconces and chandeliers amid a throng of people, held at the gaming table by a pair of beautiful eyes, and then driven from one amusement to the next – from a party to a concert, and thence to a ball – all the while frivolously paying court to a pretty blonde, then you can picture the present carnival Goethe . . . But there is another one, in a gray beaver coat with a brown silk scarf and boots, who in the sharp February wind already senses spring; whose dear wide world will soon again be open to him; who, living, striving and working tries to express the innocent feelings of youth in little poems, the powerful spices of life in a drama. It is he who can't forget you, who in the early morning suddenly feels a calling to write to you, and whose greatest happiness is to live with the best people of his age.*[84]

In early summer it seemed to Goethe *as if the threads from which my fate was hanging, which I have observed twisting to and fro for so long, finally would be woven together.*[85] To test whether he *could bear to be without Lili,*[86] he accepted an invitation from the Stolberg brothers to join them on a 'genius trip' to Switzerland. As he would at other times in his life, he attempted to weather an emotional crisis through a change in location. Dressed in 'Werther clothing', he travelled with the Stolbergs to Zürich, and from there into the Alps. Atop the Saint Gotthard Pass, faced with the choice of returning home or continuing his journey onwards toward Italy, the memory of Lili tipped the balance. Back in Frankfurt, however, he found himself in the *most unfortunate of situations.*[87] In the drama *Stella* he gave one of the characters words that likely reflected his own circumstances: *I must get away! – I would be a fool to let myself be tied down! This situation is stifling all my energy; it is sapping my soul's courage; it limits me! So much potential is in me. What couldn't still develop? – I must get away – into the wide-open world!*[88]

Farewell view toward Italy from the Gotthard, 22 June 1775. Pen and ink drawing by Goethe. He completed the drawing on top of the St. Gotthard Pass, before he turned back toward Germany.

An external catalyst brought about the separation. Some months earlier, in December 1774, Goethe had made the acquaintance of Carl August, then Hereditary Duke of Sachsen-Weimar-Eisenach, and had spent several days in his company at Mainz. When Carl August passed through Frankfurt the following autumn on the occasion of his wedding in Karlsruhe to Princess Louise of Hessen, he invited Goethe to visit Weimar and spend some time there. Goethe accepted.

Complications arose when the chamberlain who was to escort Goethe to Weimar inexplicably failed to appear as planned. *Inwardly distraught*[89] from waiting, Goethe acceded to his father's suggestion that he instead begin his long-desired journey to Italy. Thus on 30 October 1775, he set out from Frankfurt, travelling south. But when a message reached him in Heidelberg explaining the tardiness of the Duke's emissary, he changed plans and direction again, and headed east toward Weimar. In the final section of *Poetry and Truth*, he associated the situation with the workings of the *daemonic*, a mysterious power which, if *not opposed* to the moral system of the world, at least *frustrates it,*[90] and against which *all civilized forces together can do nothing.*[91] A quotation from the drama *Egmont*, on which he wrote while waiting, and in which the *daemonic* likewise was to find expression, marks the end of his youth: *Child, child! no further! As if whipped on by invisible spirits, the sun-steeds of time race on, pulling the nimble coach of our destiny behind them, and there is nothing for it but to grasp the reins courageously and try to steer, now to the right, then to the left, away from a stone here and a precipice there. Where it is going, who knows? One barely remembers whence one came.*[92]

The sentences from *Poetry and Truth*, however, are largely Goethe's reflections in his old age. To the 26-year-old who on that October day left his home town forever the *daemonic* was still a distant concept. Nonetheless he was aware of the *prophetic nature* of his situation, as evidenced in a travel log that he began a few hours before reaching Heidelberg: *Pray that your flight does not occur in winter, nor on the Sabbath, was my father's farewell warning, dispatched from his bed! This time, I riposted, without my doing it is Monday morning at six, and as far as the rest goes, the beguiling, invisible force that leads and instructs me does not ask when or what I would like. I packed for north and am heading south; I accepted and didn't go, I gave up on it and now am going! – Lili, adieu, Lili, for the second time! The first time I left still hopeful that our destinies could become entwined! It has been decided – we shall have to play our roles alone. At this time I have fears neither for you nor for me, as muddled as everything appears! – Adieu.*[93]

The First Decade in Weimar

On 7 November 1775, Goethe arrived in Weimar, then a town of barely 6,000 inhabitants and the residence of the small Duchy of Sachsen-Weimar-Eisenach. Both town and state were still under the influence of Duchess Anna Amalia, who had ruled astutely for 17 years after the premature death of her husband. Goethe later called her a *consummate princess with a consummately humane understanding*.[94] Despite the uncertainty caused there, as well as throughout all Germany, by the Seven Years War, and also despite the Duchy's limited resources, Anna Amalia had successfully promoted the arts and sciences in her realm. She created a 'Court of

Weimar from the east. Oil painting by Georg Melchior Kraus.

the Muses', with Wieland, author of the novel *Agathon* and editor of the journal *Teutscher Merkur*, a leading member. Also involved were the two chamberlains von Einsiedel, a composer, and von Seckendorff, a poet; Knebel, the erudite tutor of Anna Amalia's two sons; Musäus, a writer dubbed 'father of fairy tales'; and the publisher Bertuch. With such an *assemblage of excellent men* Anna Amalia had, in Goethe's words, *created the foundation for everything that later exerted such a lively and significant influence in this state, indeed in the entire German fatherland.*[95]

Only three months before Goethe's arrival, Carl August, Anna Amalia's older son, had come of age and succeeded her as head of state. Years later, in a conversation with Johann Peter Eckermann, Goethe reminisced about the impression that the young duke had made: *He was eighteen years old when I arrived in Weimar; but even then the buds and shoots in him gave evidence of what the tree would become. He soon attached himself closely to me and was deeply interested in everything I did. The fact that I was almost ten years older than he was beneficial for our relationship. He spent long evenings with me, deep in conversation about matters of art and nature and other worthy things. He was like a fine wine, still fermenting. He didn't know what to do with his energy, and we often came close to breaking our necks. Riding wildly over hedges and ditches, through rivers, uphill and down, wearing himself out all day long, and then camping under the wide sky at night, perhaps by a fire in the woods: that was what he liked best. Inheriting a duchy was nothing to him, but if he could have tracked one down, carried one off, or taken one by storm, that would have meant something.*[96]

It is significant that this portrait of the Duke was related only through Eckermann. A continuation of *Poetry and Truth*, in which Goethe planned to describe his first years in Weimar, never came to fruition, despite repeated urging by his friends. He himself noted that this period of his life could only be *depicted in the guise of a fable or a fairy tale; the world would never believe it for actual fact.*[97] Thus we can merely infer from letters and the observations of

Carl August. Pastel painting by Johann Heinrich Schröder, 1784. In 1775 Carl August became Duke, and in 1815 Grand Duke of Sachsen-Weimar-Eisenach. Goethe called him one of *the greatest princes Germany ever produced*.

contemporaries how Goethe's decision to spend more time at Carl August's court – so crucial for the course of his life – ripened in him. The desire to take on defined tasks certainly played a role. In February 1776 he told a confidant in Frankfurt: *I shall stay here and play my role as well as I can and as long as Fate and I take pleasure in it. Even if it were only for a few years, it is still better than the idle life I led at home, where, even though I greatly wished to, I could do nothing. Here I have several duchies to deal with. Now I am in the process of getting to know the land, which is indeed a pleasure.*[98] The *few years* that Goethe thought he would spend in Weimar turned into a lifetime. After 57 years as a resident of the city, he died there in 1832.

In June 1776, Goethe formally entered the service of the Duchy as a Privy Councillor. Carl August's admonition to his hitherto closest adviser, Fritsch, who opposed the appointment, says much about his foresight: 'Not to use a man of genius at the place where he can best employ his extraordinary talents would be to misuse him . . . With regard to public opinion, which might frown on my including Doctor Goethe in my most important council before he ever was a magistrate, a professor, a councillor or other official: it makes no difference to me. The world judges according to its prejudices, but I, like everyone who wishes to do his duty, work not just to attain fame but to be able to justify myself before God and my own conscience.'[99]

Goethe's position on the Privy Council, to which, along with the Duke, the councillors Fritsch and Schnauss belonged, brought him into contact with many aspects of governing. His tasks ranged from formulating fire-prevention regulations to maintaining relations with neighbouring courts during the Bavarian War of Succession. He took on specific assignments, such as overseeing the revival of a dormant silver mine near Ilmenau in the Thuringian Forest. In 1779 he became 'Commissioner for War', supervising the approximately 500 soldiers of the land, who were deployed mainly as guardsmen and messengers. The same year he accepted responsibility for road construction, and for dealing with floods and drainage.

This expansion of duties resulted not only from the Duke's growing confidence in him, but also from Goethe's wish to test himself in things that *might not interest hundreds of people*, yet were *absolutely necessary* for his own *education*.[100] Although initially he had merely been attracted by the idea of *trying out the role of man of affairs*,[101] by the end of 1776 he increasingly viewed his position as the equivalent of a moral test. *Main aperçu: it all boils down to ethics*[102] was the keyword he used for his activities when he later sketched an outline for the never-completed continuation of *Poetry*

Goethe's house outside Weimar, in the meadows along the Ilm River. He received the property in 1776, during his first year in Weimar, as a gift from Duke Carl August. After renovating the dilapidated house, he lived there until the spring of 1782. Even after moving into a more spacious dwelling on the Frauenplan, he often returned there.

and Truth. His diaries from the time make clear how seriously he took his responsibilities, despite both internal and external obstacles. In January 1779 he noted, for example: *Took charge of the War Commission. First session. Firm and calm in my thoughts, and sharp. Only this business in recent days. I immersed myself in it, and have good hopes for the effectiveness of persistence. The press of duties is liberating for the soul; when they have been discharged, it is freed and enjoys life. There is nothing more miserable than a person who does not try to work; he finds that loveliest of gifts to be loathsome.*[103]

In this manner, Goethe devoted himself to the *needs of the day.*[104] In 1781 he wrote to Knebel: *My nature requires me to pursue multiple tasks, and I would have to be just as busy in the smallest hamlet or on a desert island, simply in order to live, . . . for it is an article of my faith that only through steadfastness and tenacity in the present do we become worthy and able to achieve a higher stage, be it here and now or in eternity.*[105]

Apart from his administrative obligations, Goethe was drawn into activities that made use of his literary talents. Evening readings, balls and masquerades, as well as theatricals at the court were enlivened by his presence. His improvisations, which Wieland praised for their lyrical charm, have not been preserved, but published pieces reflect his efforts of the time. In 1777 he wrote the singspiel *Lila* and the theatrical whimsy *The Triumph of Sensibility*. Two other productions, *Jery and Bätely* and *The Fisherwoman*, were performed at Anna Amalia's summer residence in the park at Tiefurt. Moreover, Goethe was instrumental in bringing distinguished newcomers to Weimar: the Frankfurt painter Georg Melchior Kraus, whose watercolours convey images of Weimar and its parks, became director of the drawing academy, and Corona Schröter, a singer of great talent and warmth, joined the circle around the now Dowager Duchess Anna Amalia. In 1776, Herder accepted an appointment as head of the Duchy's churches. He and his wife Caroline, Corona Schröter, Knebel and Wieland made up the circle of Goethe's closest friends.

It was one of Anna Amalia's ladies-in-waiting, however, Charlotte von Stein, who had the most enduring impact on Goethe. Seven years older than he, her sensitivity reminded him of his sister. Raised a Calvinist and familiar with court life since childhood, she was joined in a loveless marriage with the ducal master of horses Josias von Stein. In February 1776, soon after their first encounter, Goethe confided in a letter to a Frankfurt friend: *A splendid soul is Madame von Stein, to whom I feel closely attached, no matter what people may say.*[106] He found her soothing nature increasingly indispensable. A close relationship developed, one

Charlotte von Stein at the age of 38. Silver-paint drawing, thought to be a self-portrait, about 1780. During his first ten years in Weimar, Goethe was close to Charlotte von Stein. His secretive departure for Italy caused tensions between them, and his relationship with Christiane Vulpius led to a final break. Only after 1801 did they become friendly again.

which Goethe himself found enigmatic: *I cannot explain the signif-icance, the power, that this woman has over me in any way other than by the transmigration of souls. Yes, we once were man and wife! Now we know each other – but veiled, in an ethereal aura.*[107] Unlike what he penned earlier for Lili Schönemann and later for Marianne von Willemer, the verses he wrote for Charlotte von Stein are marked by a sense of resignation. Thus in April 1776 he dedicated to her a poem addressed to an obscure future:

> *Why with insight deep did you endow us*
> *Presciently to see our future days,*
> *In despair that love will not allow us*
> *Happiness that gives us hopeful rays?*
> *Fate, why did you bless us with the feelings*
> *That should probe each other's heart and mood,*
> *That despite life's rare, tumultuous dealings*
> *We could find how our relations stood?*
>
> *Ah, so many thousands, dully drifting*
> *On through life, their own hearts barely know;*
> *To and fro they move, and idly shifting*
> *In their hopeless, unexpected woe,*
> *Then exult again when sunrise hovers*
> *With swift joys in rosy-coloured light.*
> *Only we, unfortunate two lovers,*
> *Cannot claim that mutual delight:*
> *Our love is not bare of understanding,*
> *Nor that sees the friend as he can't be,*
> *In a dream-bliss always newly landing,*
> *Even dreaming dreams so dangerously.*
>
> *Happy he in empty dreamland moving!*
> *Happy whose forebodings seem untrue!*

Every moment, every glance is proving
Dream and boding doubly for us two.
Tell me, what has fate in preparation?
Say, how could it bind us so in life?
Ah, you were in some past generation
Either sister or my wedded wife.

Every trait in me you knew, and feature,
Saw how every nerve and thought react,
With a glance you could make out my nature –
Powers that mortal eyes have often lacked.
Gave my heated blood more moderation,
Guided well my mad, wild course at length,
And my breast, distraught with desperation,
In your angel arms renewed its strength.[108]

Largely under the influence of Charlotte von Stein, Goethe began a new process of inner growth. Just as he made an effort to be thoroughgoing in his official duties, he tried to practise moderation in his personal life. He wanted to distance himself from the impulsiveness of his youth, the subjectivity of his last years in Frankfurt. Striving for *purity*[109] became the watchword he used to control his behaviour. In his diaries he measured his conduct against the desired goal, recording achievements and setbacks like a patient keeping notes on his convalescence. Thus he wrote on various days in the spring of 1778: *Was in a pleasantly resolute state;*[110] or: *Still and pure;*[111] then again: *A strange fermentation inside of me.*[112] The notation *Sad days, in solitude*[113] is followed by: *This week continually in an almost too pure mood. Good understanding about myself and our affairs, a stillness and presentiment of wisdom. A more certain feeling of having restrained myself, thereby achieving true development.*[114]

Goethe attained real calmness only when he could express his striving in literary form. In February and March 1779, when he

Corona Schröter and Goethe, as Iphigenia and Orestes in a production of the prose version of *Iphigenia in Tauris*. Oil painting by Georg Melchior Kraus, about 1779. Goethe had seen Corona Schröter on the stage in Leipzig when he was a student there. At his suggestion, Duke Carl August invited her in 1776 to introduce professionalism to the amateur theatricals in Weimar.

had to supervise army recruitment in various towns of the Duchy and also surveyed the condition of its roads, he conceived the drama *Iphigenia in Tauris*, reflecting his search for *purity*. Iphigenia's words *Only the unblemished soul is at peace*[115] echo a diary entry: *Blessed fate, let me be fresh and in control so as to attain purity.*[116] And paralleling a remark of Pylades: *To humans, the half-sullied seems pure. So strangely is this species fashioned and interrelated that no one can keep his own or others' accounts fully clean*[117] is one of Goethe's self-admonitions: *Alone, one is pure; another muddles our ideas with his own; if one listens to the third, one returns by means of the parallax to the first true meaning.*[118]

The dialogue between Thoas and Iphigenia, *Vigilant caution thwarts cunning. – And a pure soul does not need cunning. I never have, I never shall,*[119] is expressed thus in Goethe's personal experience: *And because I pay no attention to meanness, don't gossip or report on people, I often act obtusely . . . With calm and honesty everything will succeed.*[120] Even Iphigenia's plea to Thoas, *Let me perish with clean hands and a pure heart to expiate our line!*[121] is echoed in the diary: *May the concept of pureness, which extends even to the morsel I put into my mouth, become ever more lucid in me.*[122]

The period after Goethe wrote *Iphigenia*, especially the summer of 1779, was a decisive phase of his development before he journeyed to Italy. Not only the fact that he had given literary expression to his yearning for purity, but also the sense that he was more competent in his official duties contributed to his deepening self-understanding. When emergencies occurred, such as fires in the villages of the Duchy or flooding along the Ilm and the Saale rivers, he acted with a newfound composure: *Wanted on Sunday the 25th [of July] to go to Berka. During the night a violent fire broke out in Apolda; I went there early in the morning, as soon as I heard about it, and was roasted and steamed all day . . . My plans, thoughts and schedule were burnt, too, to some extent. Life goes on thus to its end; others will have the same experience after us. My ideas about fire prevention confirmed again. And especially those about local conditions, where one can only play the game, as with everything, with the cards one holds at the moment. My eyes are burning from the embers and the smoke, and the soles of my feet ache. Misery is gradually becoming as prosaic to me as*

Burning village, by night. Chalk drawing by Goethe, dating from his early years in Weimar. Supervision of firefighting during the frequent village fires was one of Goethe's responsibilities. The drawing gives no indication of the location or date of the fire, but it may have occurred on 16 April 1776, when Goethe noted in his diary: *At the fire in Ulrichshalben, where 21 houses and a man were incinerated.*

Blest is one who with a heart
Free of bitterness
Shuns the world and lives apart
In a friend's embrace,

There to learn, if learn we can,
What unknown delight
Through the labyrinth-soul of man
Wanders in the night.

Closing verses of the poem *To the Moon*. Translated by David Luke, in Johann Wolfgang von Goethe, *Selected Poetry* (London: 1999)

a hearth fire. But I shan't let go of my thoughts and I shall struggle with the unknown angel, even though I might dislocate my joints.[123]

The more prosaic Goethe's tasks seemed to him, the more he strove for order and consistency. *Order,*[124] which he now understood to include the previously all-important purity, appeared from the beginning of 1780 to be the criterion for his self-examination. *Worked on getting things done.*[125] – *Took care of business well. Daily routine calm and pure. Took up organisation of the War Commission again. I haven't been able to achieve this yet in a year and a half! I will do it! And I want to do it as if pigeons had been picking it clean.*[126] – *Daily more order, certainty and results.*[127] A letter to Lavater from September 1780 illustrates his convictions: *The work with which I have been charged, and which each day becomes easier and more difficult, requires my presence waking and dreaming. This responsibility becomes daily more precious to me, and I hope to equal the greatest men in this and in nothing higher. This yearning to raise the peak of the pyramid of my existence, the base of which was laid out for me, as far into the air as possible outweighs everything else and barely allows me to forget it for a moment.*[128]

Out of the daily demands a new crisis was developing. After Goethe returned from a journey to Switzerland with Duke Carl August in the autumn of 1779, he was overcome by the feeling that he was *less able to prevail against the many things*[129] that required his attention. While he was gaining *ever more knowledge and competence for an active life*, he also felt *like a bird that has become entangled in twine: I have wings, but I cannot use them.*[130] Activities in

Goethe's manuscript of the poem *To the Moon*. He enclosed it in a letter to Charlotte von Stein on 18 January 1778.

which he had previously wanted to *bathe*[131] began to cost him some effort. To Charlotte von Stein he wrote: *How much happier I would be if I were isolated from the squabbles of political factions and could devote my mind to the sciences and arts, to which I was born.*[132] In such a mood, in February 1780 he *invented*[133] the drama *Tasso*, the message of which he identified as *the disproportion between talent and life.*[134] He seemed increasingly to be noticing such a disproportion in his own existence. Typical of his attitude from about 1780 onward was the remark that he had *stuck to daily tasks*.[135] In a letter to Johann Friedrich Krafft, a man impoverished as a result of unfortunate circumstances and in despair about his situation, whom Goethe had supported for several years from his own pocket, he wrote: *'Must' is a harsh word, but only when dealing with this 'must' can one show what one is made of. Anyone can live wilfullly*.[136]

Despite such renunciation, Goethe's early years in Weimar were not lost ones with regard to artistic creativitity. He completed the prose version of *Iphigenia* and the beginning of *Wilhelm Meister's Apprenticeship*. A draft of *Tasso* and several components of *Faust* can be traced to this period. Judging not by the size of his production but by its significance, these were fruitful years for his lyrics, as well. One winter night when the Ilm flooded the meadows around his house, he conceived the poem *To the Moon*. On top of the Kickelhahn, a wooded mountain above the town of Ilmenau, he scratched into the wall of a hunting lodge a verse with the first lines *O'er all the hill-tops is quiet now*, and during a ride to Goslar in December 1777 he drafted *Harz Journey in Winter*. His involvement in his duties provided the background for the poems *Boundaries of Mankind* and *The Divine*.

Externally, Goethe achieved many successes. When he was put in charge of the Duchy's financial authority, all crucial offices of the land were in his hands. In June 1782, he was raised by Emperor Joseph II to the nobility. At almost the same time, he gave up his house in the meadows along the Ilm and moved to a more spacious residence in the centre of town.

He began to pursue extensive studies in the sciences. Supervision of the mine near Ilmenau had forced him to involve himself in geological and mineralogical matters. Contacts at the university in Jena stimulated his interest in comparative anatomy. Convinced that all forms of life are interrelated, in 1784 he proved the existence in humans of the intermaxillary bone, previously thought to be present only in animals. Almost a century before Darwin, his work suggested a theory of biological evolution.

The pleasure Goethe took in his studies of nature reminded him of the extent to which he had neglected his own interests for the sake of his administrative duties. Thus at the end of his tenth year in Weimar, he reached a decision to distance himself from his obligations there, if only temporarily. After putting all his official and personal affairs in order, he asked the Duke for an *indefinite leave of absence*.[137] His actual departure took place seemingly from one day to the next and, as earlier in 1772 in Wetzlar and 1775 in Frankfurt, resembled a flight. He informed no one, not even the Duke or Charlotte von Stein, about his specific plans. After a brief stay in Bohemia, he began the most momentous journey of his life: *Early on 3 September [1786] at three in the morning I stole out of Carlsbad; otherwise, I should not have been allowed to go, even though people were aware that I wanted to leave. I would not let myself be deterred, for it was time.*[138]

Italian Journey

Calling himself 'Philipp Möller, merchant', Goethe took the mail coach south from Carlsbad. In a travel log he meticulously recorded his observations: *Crossing into Bavaria one comes upon Waldsassen Abbey, situated in a lovely meadow and surrounded by fertile rolling hills. The soil is decomposed argillaceous slate, made friable by the quartz that was contained in the slate but did not break down. Until Tirschenreuth the land climbs, and the streams flow toward one in the direction of the Eger and Elbe rivers; beyond Tirschenreuth the land slopes southward, and the streams run toward the Danube.*[139]

The notes from his logbook illustrate the manner in which Goethe attempted throughout his journey to study his surroundings: he no longer wished *to reflect, feel, fantasize,*[140] as he had done earlier, but *to see the objects with my own eyes,*[141] to observe inquisitively landscapes and works of art, and give clear accounts of them: *I tried as much as possible to forget my previous approach and to comprehend only the object itself, in its own purity.*[142]

By way of Regensburg, Innsbruck and the Brenner Pass, Goethe reached Italian soil at Trento after a week of strenuous travelling: *I feel as if I had been born and raised here, and were just coming back from a journey to Greenland, from a whaling expedition. Everything is welcome to me.*[143] When he was surrounded by the southern landscape at Lake Garda, he retrieved from his luggage the prose manuscript of *Iphigenia* and began – as he had long planned – to transform it into iambs. In Verona's amphitheatre he gazed for the first time at a building from classical antiquity. He travelled on to Vicenza, where he was fascinated by Palladio's palatial structures,

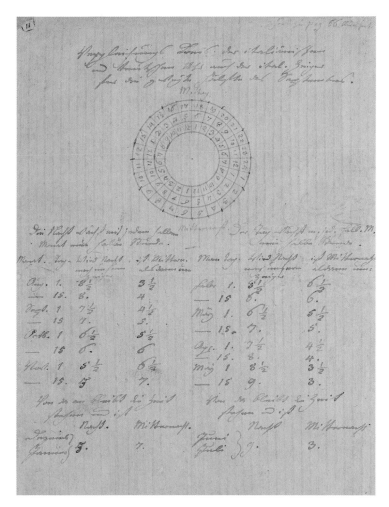

Diagram and table comparing German and Italian times. Enclosure in the travel log that Goethe kept for Charlotte von Stein. Verona, 17 September 1786.

and then to Venice: *In the Book of Fate it was written on my page that in 1786, on the twenty-eighth of September at five in the afternoon, coming from the Brenta to the lagoons I should first view Venice, and should soon thereafter disembark and visit this wonderful island city.*[144]

Two weeks later, he left Venice behind. At Bologna he decided: *I shall simply pass through Florence and go straight to Rome. I can take no pleasure in anything until that need has been stilled.*[145] On 29 October 1786 he reached his goal: *At last I have arrived in this capital of the world! . . . Now I am here and tranquil, and it seems as if I am content with my whole existence. One can truly say a new life begins when one sees everything with one's own eyes that in part one already knows inside out. All the dreams of my youth are coming true; the first copperplates that I remember I see now in reality, and everything that has been familiar to me in paintings and drawings, etchings and woodcuts, in plaster and in cork, now is assembled before me. Wherever I go, I find acquaintances in a new world; everything is the way I thought it would be, and everything is new.*[146]

Goethe's first stay in Rome lasted four months. He spent almost all his time surveying works of art. As he looked at the *colossal yet refined proportions*, he felt like *a witness to the great decrees of Fortune.*[147] To Charlotte von Stein he wrote: *I take in everything and don't try to find anything specific in an object. As I earlier observed nature, now I observe art; I am gaining what I long desired, and also a more complete concept of the highest accomplishments of humankind, and my soul, learning increasingly, finds a more expansive domain.*[148]

Along with Rome's art and the southern landscape, the vitality of the Italians appealed to Goethe. He attended theatre performances and judicial proceedings, observed processions and church ceremonies. After the way he had lived during the preceding years, such experiences were exhilarating. He felt as if he were *daily shedding another skin*,[149] indeed, as if he were experiencing a *change extending into the very marrow of my bones.*[150] In his letters he spoke of a *rebirth* that was transfiguring him *from the inside outwards.*[151] He felt unreservedly *happy.*[152] To his friends in Weimar he reported: *I have finally achieved the goal of my desire and live here in a clarity and tranquillity that you can imagine, knowing me. My*

View from Monte Pincio toward Rome, with the church of San Carlo al Corso and the Vatican. Pencil and ink drawing by Goethe, February 1787. During the year and a half of his stay in Italy, Goethe executed many drawings in this style, also a number of watercolours, in all more than 900 pieces.

practise of seeing and reading all things as they are, my fidelity to viewing with a clear eye, my total lack of pretension, are making me deeply happy. Every day brings a marvelous new object, every day great new, incredible images, and a whole of which one has long thought and dreamt, but never attained in the imagination.[153]

Goethe's *total lack of pretension* surprised those who encountered him. The painter Wilhelm Tischbein, in whose house he took up lodgings, wrote to Lavater: 'Goethe was somewhat known to me through you and other friends, and I have found him to be as I thought. What I didn't anticipate was so much gravity and ease in the lively man of feeling. I am also delighted by his simple way of life. He sought from me a small room where he could sleep and work undisturbed, and modest meals, which I can easily provide, as he is content with so little. So there he sits, and writes in the mornings, trying to complete his Iphigenia, and then he goes out and contemplates the city's art.'[154]

From February to June 1787, Goethe undertook a trip to the southern part of the country. While in Naples he visited excavations at Pompeii and the temples at Paestum, whose *massive, truncated, bevelled columns, all crowded together,* at first struck him as *disturbing, even frightful.*[155] Only after recalling Winckelmann's concept of the *severe* style of sculpture could he *feel reconciled*[156] to these monuments of Greek architecture. He climbed Mount Vesuvius three times and observed at close hand the *hellishly seething cauldron.*[157] Together with the painter Christoph Kniep, who instructed him in the use of watercolours, he travelled by packet boat to Sicily. Without knowledge of the island, he thought, one could not form a true image of Italy: *here is the key to everything.*[158] In Taormina and Messina he spent days immersed in Homer and felt the *Odyssey come alive.*[159] A plan for a tragedy about Odysseus' encounter with Nausicaa occupied him so intensively that in retrospect it seemed to him as if he had *dreamt away the greater part of the Sicilian journey*[160].

He also made progress in his study of nature. Having already *given careful consideration*[161] to the laws governing all plant and animal development, observations in the public gardens of Palermo helped him arrive at his concept of a *primal plant*, in which he believed he had discovered the principle of the *original identity of all parts of the plant.*[162] To Herder he wrote: *The primal plant will be the most singular creation in the world, for which nature itself should envy me. With this model, and the key to it, one can invent an endless number of plants that will have to be consistent with each other: those which don't exist, could exist, and are not just artistic or literary shades and apparitions, but have an inner truth and necessity. The same law will apply to all other living things.*[163]

Goethe gazing out of the window in his Roman lodging at the Corso, the street two storeys below him. Watercolour and chalk on pencil, by Wilhelm Tischbein, 1787. During Goethe's stay in Rome, Tischbein portrayed him on several occasions. His life-size oil painting *Goethe in the Campagna* has frequently been reproduced, most famously by Andy Warhol, who appropriated a segment of it for a poster.

After his return from southern Italy, Goethe stayed in Rome for almost another year. This *second Roman sojourn*[164] was a time of intensive and steady work. He produced drawings almost daily, completed the drama *Egmont* and the version of *Iphigenia* in iambs, continued to write on *Tasso* and penned a depiction of the *Roman Carnival*. With the composer Philipp Kayser he discussed plans for an *Egmont Symphony*[165] and listened to medieval church music. He spent two idyllic weeks in Castel Gandolfo, south of Rome, among a circle of friends around the English painter Thomas Jenkins and the *beautiful Milanese*[166] Maddalena Riggi. His recollections of her in the *Italian Journey*, as well as references in the *Roman Elegies* to a woman named Faustina, are indicative of an awakening sensuality that he had barely seemed to evince before his departure from Germany.

Parade of the Pulcinello King. Illustration for *The Roman Carnival*, coloured copperplate by Georg Melchior Kraus, 1789. Goethe's report on this event, which he had observed in February 1788, came out the following year, in a deluxe edition by the Berlin publisher Unger.

Above all else, he continued to work on his understanding of art. Tirelessly he visited monuments, galleries and museums. As during his first Roman sojourn, artists and scholars of art were his companions: Tischbein, Philipp Hackert, Angelika Kauffmann, Karl Philipp Moritz. He became close to the *quiet, retiring, hardworking*[167] painter Heinrich Meyer, from Zürich. Yet Meyer's influence – *he steadily followed the path that had been forged by Winckelmann*[168] – proved to be unfortunate, as it was mainly he who, after later settling in Weimar, kept Goethe from turning his attention to any work of art that was not strictly classical.

Leaving Rome was painful. Years later, in 1829, when he was dictating the closing chapter of his *Italian Journey*, Goethe remembered vividly how in the days before his departure he had wandered through the city, the last time in bright moonlight: *After several enjoyable, sometimes also stressful days, I finally made my rounds alone. Having hiked the long Corso, I climbed the Capitoline Hill, which stood there like a fairy palace in the desert. Farther on, completely dark and casting even darker shadows, the victory arch of Septimius Severus stood before me. In the loneliness of the Via Sacra the buildings, usually so familiar, seemed strange and ghostly. And as I neared the noble ruins of the Colosseum and peered through the grating into the interior, I can't deny that a shiver ran through me and hastened my departure.*[169]

Evolution, not Revolution

The return to Weimar brought disappointments. Although Goethe had tried to inform friends who stayed behind not only about his new experiences but about his inner development, as well, once at home he did not succeed in renewing the relationships: *From Italy, so rich in form, I came back to shapeless Germany, where I had to exchange a bright sky for a gloomy one. My friends, instead of embracing and comforting me, drove me to despair. My enthusiasm for things far away and barely familiar to them, my sorrow, my laments over what I had lost, seemed to offend them; I received no sympathy, no one understood my language.*[170]

Goethe felt isolated. Duke Carl August, with whom it would have been easiest to reestablish contact, was often away, discharging his duties as a general in the Prussian army. Herder, aware that he had lost his previous influence over Goethe, withdrew morosely. And Charlotte von Stein was still upset about his secretive departure. Despite his beseeching pleas[171] that she help ease his return, she received him without heart,[172] seemingly no longer willing to understand him. Thus at the beginning of 1789, it came to a breach. Instead of looking in Weimar for company, Goethe sought it among professors at the university in Jena, and he appointed Heinrich Meyer to a position at the ducal drawing academy. He occasionally encountered Schiller, then already a highly respected writer, who lived in nearby Rudolstadt, but they did not warm to each other. Schiller suggested that this was due to their different 'views of the world': Goethe's thought was based too much 'on the materiality of objects', while his own 'relied on sensation'.[173] In personal terms, he felt rebuffed: 'To be often in Goethe's company would not make me happy. Even with his closest friends he doesn't open up; one can't pin him down. I think, in fact, he is an egotist to an unusual degree. He has a talent for fascinating people and obliging them with small or large courtesies; but he always manages to keep himself aloof. One should not tolerate this kind of person. I find him to be like a condescending prude, whom one has to get with child in order to humiliate her before the world.'[174]

Schiller's views may have been influenced by gossip that was spreading in Weimar about Goethe's domestic circumstances. The simple fact was that barely a month after his return from Rome, he took as his mistress a 23-year-old woman, Christiane Vulpius, who had attracted him with the openness of her personality. She soon moved into his house. He described the bond with the words *I am married, just not by means of a ceremony*[175] and found much joy in it, despite the calumny making the rounds in the city. Of the five children Christiane bore him, only the

Christiane Vulpius asleep on a sofa. Pencil drawing by Goethe, 1788 or 1789.

Christiane Vulpius came from a middle-class family in Weimar. Orphaned as a young girl, she was employed in a business that produced artificial flowers. On 12 June 1788 she approached Goethe in the park along the Ilm with a petition from her brother Christian August Vulpius. That was the prelude to her relationship with Goethe, both out of wedlock and in, which lasted until her death in 1816.

first, a son – August – born in 1789, lived beyond infancy. Poetic testimony to their loving relationship are the sensual *Roman Elegies*, in which Christiane's features are melded with those of the Roman Faustina.

After 1788, Goethe resumed his earlier administrative duties on only a limited basis. He remained a nominal member of the Privy Council, but focused his attention on the scientific and artistic institutions of the Duchy, particularly the university at Jena. He devoted himself energetically to the Weimar court theatre, founded in 1791, and within a few years developed it into one of the most respected stages in Germany. Yet he was disappointed by the public, who showed more interest in light pieces by Iffland and Kotzebue, forgotten today, than in his own or Schiller's plays.

During this period he produced only a few literary works: the *Roman Elegies*, the *Venetian Epigrams*, some occasional poetry for the Weimar theatre and a version in hexameter of the chapbook *Reynard the Fox*. Rather than to literature, he felt drawn *more than ever to the sciences*.[176] He tirelessly conducted botanical, anatomical and optical experiments. Building on his earlier concept of the primal plant, he proposed a system of all plant development, which he called *The Metamorphosis of Plants*. In this small work, printed in 1790, he tried to prove that all parts of a plant can be traced back to a single basic organ, the leaf that grows out of the node. Mature plants are formed in a process of gradual transformation, and diversity can be explained by means of variations in this process of metamorphosis: *Whether the plant sprouts, blooms or bears fruit, it is always the same elements that, in numerous designs and often in altered form, follow the rules of nature. The element that on the stem expands into a leaf, which can assume any number of shapes, also contracts in the calyx and expands again into a flower petal, and contracts into a reproductive organ to expand one last time as a fruit.*[177]

Goethe developed similar concepts in osteology. When he travelled to Venice in the spring of 1790 to meet Dowager Duchess Anna Amalia on her return from a sojourn in Italy, a sheep's skeleton on the Lido led him to discover that cranial bones in both animals and humans originate in related vertebrae. From this point it was just a step to the theory of morphology that he would develop in the coming years: all matter is *in motion, becoming, decaying: the theory of matter is the theory of evolution.*[178]

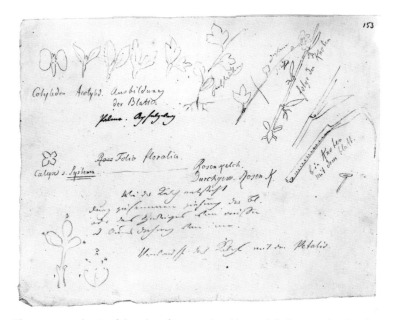

The metamorphosis of the plant from seed to bloom. Ink drawing by Goethe, after 1790. The caption reads: *How the calyx originates in the contraction of the leaves or the twig externally and expansion internally. Relationship of the calyx to the petal.*

Related to Goethe's scientific studies was his stance toward the French Revolution. Although he had long been concerned about the *immoral abyss of city, court and state* under Bourbon rule,[179] his attitude was determined by his conviction that, as in nature, changes in society take place by means of evolution. In contrast to the enthusiasm with which the storming of the Bastille was welcomed by contemporaries such as Schiller, Klopstock and even Herder, Goethe felt that the unleashing of revolutionary instincts endangered any intellectual culture. In two plays completed between 1791 and 1793, *The Citizen General* and *The Agitated*, he distanced himself from the concept that political grievances can be redressed through violence. As a result, he was reproached for showing no interest in the cause of freedom. Still defending himself much later, in a conversation with Eckermann in 1824, he noted: *It is true, I could be no friend of the French Revolution, for its horrors incensed and shocked me daily and hourly, while its beneficial consequences were not yet apparent. I also could not be indifferent to the fact that others in Germany were endeavouring artificially to bring about events similar to those in France, where they were the consequence of an enormous necessity . . . I was convinced that a great revolution is never the fault of the people, but of the government. Revolutions are impossible if governments are just and continually alert, preventing unrest by initiating reforms, instead of resisting until their necessity is forced upon them from below.*[180]

Goethe was personally affected by events in the summer of 1792, when the united armies of Austria and Prussia opened a campaign against France's revolutionary forces. At the request of Duke Carl August, who commanded a Prussian regiment, he joined his retinue. Almost 30 years later he wrote about his experiences in the autobiographical piece *Campaign in France*. With its depiction of military events interwoven with personal thoughts on *existing between order and disorder, between survival and ruin, between stealing and paying,*[181] it reflects the attitude of the observer, who hardly evinced soldierly passions. During the bombardment of Verdun, his interest was directed to a pond in which tiny fish created prismatic effects. And during the Allies' fateful attempt on 19 September 1792 to achieve an opening toward Paris by advancing near Valmy, he seemed to notice the physical effects of the cannonade rather than the events of war. But as the futility of the efforts became apparent, it was he in particular who foresaw how the day's developments presaged the fall of the Holy Roman Empire: *The greatest consternation spread throughout the army. That very morning one had thought of nothing else but skewering the French and serving them up on a platter. Now, however, everyone went his own way, without looking others in the eye, or, if one did, it was to swear or curse. As night was falling, by chance we had formed a circle, although we could not light the customary fire. Most were quiet, a few talked, but no one really had anything reasonable to say. Finally I was asked what I thought about the state of affairs, for I had usually entertained the group with little stories. Now I said: Here, today, a new epoch in world history has begun, and you can say that you were present.*[182]

Contemporary Events, 1789–1801

1789 French Revolution

1790 Death of Emperor Joseph II

1792 French National Assembly's declaration of war against Austria

1792 Allied armies of Austria and Prussia cross the Rhine, retreat after the bombardment at Valmy

1793 Seige of French-occupied Mainz by the allies. Withdrawal of the French army

1795 Peace concluded between France and Prussia

1798–1801 Second war against France waged by a coalition of Austria, England and Russia

1799 Napoleon assumes control of France as First Consul

Following the withdrawal of the allied armies, Goethe returned to Weimar by way of Düsseldorf and Münster. Prolonged visits with Jacobi in the former city and Princess Amalie Gallitzin in the latter helped him to put his French experiences into perspective. Once more, however, he became a witness to war, again in the entourage of Duke Carl August, when the allies laid siege to French-occupied Mainz in the following summer. An episode that occurred after the bombardment and surrender of the city on 22 July 1793 is revealing for Goethe's way

Goethe at the age of 42. Copperplate by Johann Heinrich Lips after a chalk drawing. Goethe met the artist first in Zürich, then in Rome. In 1789 he supported the appointment of Lips to a position at the Drawing Institute in Weimar.

of thinking. As he was watching the withdrawal of French troops near a guardhouse, a group of locals threatened to attack a hated collaborator, who, along with his family, was about to leave the city under a safe-conduct. Calling upon his authority as an associate of the Duke of Weimar, Goethe vigorously dispersed the angry crowd and cleared a path for the fugitives. The incident led to a conversation with the English painter Charles Gore, who had witnessed it: *When I met up with friend Gore afterward, he rebuked me in his English-French: What bug bit you? You got involved in a business that could have gone badly. I wasn't frightened, I responded; and don't*

you find it more pleasant that I kept the area so clean? How would it look now if it were full of rubbish, which would annoy everyone – even if that chap did not deserve the possessions he so blithely carried off...
Meanwhile, the good Gore was still unhappy that I had put myself in danger and risked so much, all for an unknown, perhaps criminal individual. I kept referring lightheartedly to the clean area before the guardhouse, but at last said impatiently: It is simply my nature – I would rather commit an injustice than tolerate disorder.[183]

Goethe expressly repeated these words in his report on *The Siege of Mainz*. They indicate how the behaviour of an emotional crowd disturbed the scientist who believed in an organic development of all living things. Both revolutionary and nationalistic slogans dismayed him, much to the indignation of some contemporaries. For himself, he felt, in politically unsettled times it was best to *stick to his quiet study* and *carefully preserve the holy fire of science and art, even if it is only an ember under the ashes, so that when the night of war has passed and the dawn of peace is breaking, the indispensable Promethean fire will not have vanished.*[184]

Friendship with Schiller

Goethe was liberated from the isolation into which he had fallen after his Italian journey by an encounter with Schiller. Later he often mentioned how consequential this *happy event*[185] was for him, although not without noting the obstacles that had hindered an earlier accord. The *ethical and theatrical paradoxes* which Schiller's drama *The Robbers* had *poured over the fatherland in full rapturous flood*[186] had been contrary to his own views, and even Schiller's appreciation of *Werther* had disgruntled rather than gratified him. However, due to an intensive study of Kant, Schiller had undergone a transformation in the early 1790s that was comparable to the effect on Goethe of his journey to Italy.

Independent endeavours by the two men to develop normative concepts of art favoured a rapprochement. It occurred seemingly *by chance*[187] at the end of July 1794, after a meeting of the Jena Scientific Society: *We began to converse; he [Schiller] appeared to have found the session worthwhile, but observed with insight that such an unintegrated approach to nature might not appeal to the interested layman. I responded that it might be unappealing even for the initiated and that there could be a different way to present nature: not as separate and isolated, but as vibrant and alive, achieving a totality from its various parts. He desired to be enlightened about this, although he didn't conceal his doubts. He could not agree that what I asserted could come from experience. We reached his house, and the conversation drew me inside. There I gave a lively presentation on the metamorphosis of plants, with a few strokes of the pen causing a symbolic plant to grow before his eyes. He listened carefully and observed every-thing with great interest. But when I was done, he shook his head and said: that is not an experience, it is an idea. I was taken aback, some-what annoyed: this was the issue that separated us, clearly delineated. The old resentment began to stir, but I controlled myself and responded: It appeals to me that I have ideas without knowing it and even see them with my own eyes.*[188]

Schiller, around 1793–1794. Lithograph by Siegfried Bendiken after a pastel by Ludovike Simanowitz.

It was Schiller who, after this amicable contact, took the next step. In a letter that testifies to what Goethe later called his *wisdom and civility*,[189] he laid the groundwork for the friendship that soon developed. When he wrote this letter, he was 35 and Goethe 45 years old: 'I have long watched, although from some distance, with ever renewed admiration the trajectory of your intellect and the course that you have marked out for yourself. You seek necessity in nature, but you seek it using the most difficult approach, one which a lesser mind would not even attempt. You look at nature as a whole and try to find clarification about its separate parts. From a simple organism you proceed, step by step, to the more sophisticated, finally to build the most complex, the human being, genetically from the materials of all nature. By re-creating man in this way, you attempt to penetrate his hidden mechanisms. A grand and truly heroic idea, that demonstrates the degree to which your intellect binds together the rich aggregate of its concepts in a beautiful unity . . . This is how I dare to judge the course of your mind, and you yourself will know best whether I am right.'[190]

Goethe's answer followed four days later. In it he openly showed his appreciation: *For my birthday, which occurs this week, no gift could have been more welcome than your letter, in which with a friendly hand you draw the sum of my existence and with your interest encourage me to a more diligent and lively use of my talents . . . I shall gladly share whatever concerns my outer and inner self. Because I am acutely aware that my undertakings far exceed the measure of human capabilities and their earthly duration, I should like to deposit some thoughts with you, not only to preserve them but also to give them new life.*[191]

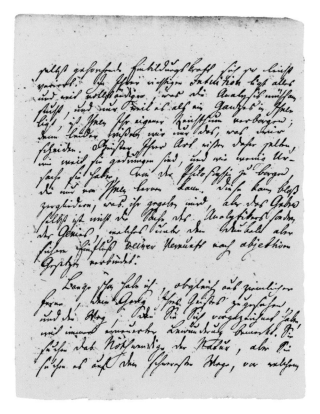

Page from Schiller's letter to Goethe of 23 August 1794. The lower paragraph ('I have long watched...') is reproduced on page 69.

Goethe's and Schiller's *first encounter*[192] gave rise to an intensive exchange of ideas that brought both men *pure pleasure and real benefit*.[193] Goethe moderated Schiller's tendency toward *philosophical speculation*,[194] and Schiller drew Goethe away from his scientific studies towards more literary efforts. In 1794 Goethe contributed *Conversations among German Emigrants* to Schiller's journal *The Horae* and agreed to publish portions of his *Roman Elegies*. When *The Horae* elicited only a modest response, the two authors collaborated on almost a thousand epigrams, the *Xenien*, in which they gave free rein to their irritation with the public in general and contentious reviewers in particular. Schiller called the collection, published in 1796 in the *Muses' Almanach*, a 'wild, godless satire, intermingled with flashes of poetic and philosophical inspiration.'[195]

The 'Xenien year' was followed by a 'ballad year'. Buoyed by their interest in each other's efforts, Goethe and Schiller completed a series of lengthy ballads, including *The Bride of Corinth*, *The Sorcerer's Apprentice* and *The God and the Bayadere* by the former, *The Diver* and *The Cranes of Ibycus* by the latter. Beginning in 1796, Schiller worked on his *Wallenstein* trilogy. Goethe completed *Wilhelm Meister's Apprenticeship,* the novel he had begun many years earlier. He also resumed work on *Faust*, which he had set aside after his return from Italy. Influenced by contemporary events, he wrote the epic *Hermann and Dorothea*. Its amiable and idyllic descriptions of Germany's bourgeoisie made him a popular author again for the first time since the appearance of *Werther*.

In an extensive correspondence, the two attempted to formulate a set of classicistic principles. Goethe's quest in his scientific studies for principles underlying changes in appearance was now extended to poetry and art. Harmony, self-perfection, devotion to 'the True, the Beautiful, the Good', and the model afforded by antiquity were felt to form the basis for a noble and balanced culture. Inner harmony was to be matched by an elegance of form.

Over the years, the collaboration between the two became so intensive that Goethe felt he was experiencing *a new springtime, in which everything sprouted happily together, arising out of newly opened seeds and twigs.*[196] In order to take greater advantage of the opportunities afforded by their contacts, Schiller gave up his academic position in Jena and moved in 1799 to Weimar. This provided new impetus to Goethe's efforts in the theatre there. Productions of Schiller's *Maria Stuart* (1800), *The Bride of Messina* (1803) and *Wilhelm Tell* (1804), as well as Calderón's and Shakespeare's

Schiller, the Humboldt brothers and Goethe in Jena. Xylograph by W. Aarland, 1797. Between 1794 and 1797, both Wilhelm and Alexander von Humboldt made frequent visits to Jena and became friends with Schiller, then also with Goethe. In his *Daily and Annual Agendas* for 1797, Goethe noted: *The Humboldt brothers were here, and all of nature was discussed from the perspectives of philosophy and of science.*

dramas in translations by August Wilhelm Schlegel, provided occasions to test out the classisistic principles of style that Goethe and Schiller had developed. Not least because of these activities, the small residence attracted increasing attention as a centre of German intellectual life. Wilhelm and Alexander von Humboldt, Fichte, Schelling and Hegel visited Weimar or established contact from Jena. Decidedly critical dialogues developed with the German Romantics, first in the area of the visual arts. The agendas of the Weimar Art Friends, drawn up jointly by Goethe, Schiller and Meyer, met with opposition from the younger generation. Characteristic was the protest voiced in 1802 by Philipp Otto Runge, then 24 years old, against the restriction of the Weimar Annual Art Competition to motifs from antiquity: 'The exhibition in Weimar and the whole operation there are gradually moving in a totally wrong direction, where it will be impossible to produce anything good. We are no longer Greeks; we can no longer feel that environment when we see their consummate works of art, much less produce such works ourselves; and why should we exert ourselves to turn out something mediocre?'[197]

Since 1794, few events in Goethe's life had not been associated with Schiller, and only two journeys – to Switzerland in 1797, and to Bad Pyrmont and Göttingen in 1801 – had taken him any distance from Weimar. But in 1805 the friendship came to an abrupt end. Both Schiller and Goethe had been unwell from January onwards, and their usual exchange of thoughts had become almost impossible. Schiller no longer had much hope that he would recover from his chronic ailments. Goethe wrote later about this period: *Meanwhile, two frightful events, two fires that occurred within just a few nights of each other endangering me personally both times, caused a relapse of the ailment from which I had been trying to recuperate. Schiller felt himself similarly trapped. Our personal meetings were suspended; we exchanged hasty notes. Some that he wrote in February and March give evidence of his suffering, of his activities and of his increasingly flagging hope. At the beginning of May I ventured out; I found him just about to leave for the theatre and didn't want to detain him. Some discomfort kept me from accompanying him, and so we parted in front of his house, never to see each other again.*[198] Schiller died on 9 May 1805.

Following Schiller's death, Goethe felt as if he existed in a *hollow void*. He went about his daily activities *by rote*, letting himself *be led by them, instead of leading them.*[199] In a letter to the Berlin building contractor and composer Carl Friedrich Zelter, to whom he was becoming increasingly attached, drawn by Zelter's unaffected nature, he noted: *Since last I wrote, I have had few good days. I thought*

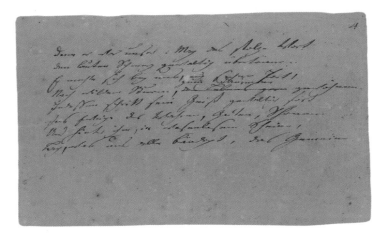

The fourth stanza of the *Epilogue to Schiller's Bell*, in Goethe's hand:

> For he was ours: May those words of pride
> Drown out our clamourous cries of lamentation!
> In our safe port, secure from storm and tide,
> He well could seek his lasting habitation.
> Meanwhile his titan soul did forward stride,
> In Goodness, Truth and Beauty found duration.
> Behind him lay, to empty shadows faded,
> The mean and base, which keeps us all degraded.

Translation by Edwin H. Zeydel, in *Goethe, the Lyrist* (Chapel Hill: 1955).

to lose my own life, and instead have lost a friend, and with him the half of my existence. In truth, I should begin a new way of life; but at my age that is no longer possible. So I simply live one day at a time and do the next thing that needs to be done, without looking further ahead.[200]

Goethe was able to recover from his illness, a painful renal colic that had worsened after Schiller's death, by undergoing treatment at Bad Lauchstädt, a spa near Halle. When the summer theatre there was rehearsing a dramatic version of Schiller's popular *Song of the Bell*, he wrote an *Epilogue* to the poem, using the words *For he was ours!* as a refrain.[201] However, he gave up the idea of a public memorial, still too much affected by the course of events. An attempt to complete the fragment of a *Demetrius* drama left behind by Schiller came to nought. Not until 1826 was Goethe able to produce a personal obituary: after observing Schiller's remains when they were removed from a vault at the St. Jacob Cemetery and kept in the ducal library prior to final interment, he wrote *Lines on Seeing Schiller's Skull*.[202]

The Napoleonic Years

Contemporary Events, 1805–1815

1805 Battle of the Three Emperors, near Austerlitz: Napoleon defeats Austria and Russia

1806–1807 France wages war against Prussia and Russia

1806 Battle of Jena and Auerstedt: Napoleon vanquishes the Prussian army

1806 Francis II relinquishes the Imperial crown. Dissolution of the Holy Roman Empire of the German Nation

1812 Napoleon's campaign against Russia. Burning of Moscow, retreat of the French

1813–1815 German Wars of Liberation

1813 Battle of the Nations, near Leipzig

1814–1815 Congress of Vienna. Sachsen-Weimar-Eisenach elevated to a Grand Duchy

1815 Battle of Waterloo: Wellington's and Blücher's victory over Napoleon. Napoleon exiled to St. Helena

With the death of Schiller, Goethe perceived an era in his life coming to an end. This awareness was reinforced by political developments. Having in 1792 predicted the collapse of the Holy Roman Empire, he found the French invasion of Germany in 1806 to be a *violent interruption* of a culture that had evolved during a *long era of peace*,[203] but unlike many others he hardly considered it a catastrophe. In his view, the future of the German nation lay in the arts and sciences, not in politics. Even 24 years later, when Eckermann questioned him about his stance during the period of Napoleonic rule, he responded in the same vein. Eckermann reported: 'People have blamed you,' I began somewhat undiplomatically, 'for not taking up arms or at least trying to use your influence as an author during that great time.' *Let us drop that, my friend!* Goethe responded. *This is an absurd world, which doesn't know what it wants. One has to allow it to talk and to have its own way. – How could I have taken up arms without hatred! And how could I have hated without being young! If these events had occurred when I was a 20-year-old, I surely would not have been the last to get involved; however, they found me already beyond my first 60 years . . . To write war songs sitting in a room! In a bivouac, where one nightly hears the horses of enemy outposts neighing: I could have done that. But that was not my life nor was it to my taste, although it was Theodor Körner's. His war songs become him perfectly. For me, not being of a bellicose nature, war songs would have been a mask that would have ill suited me.*[204]

Even when he was personally drawn into the turmoil of war, Goethe tried to maintain his distance. Almost like a neutral observer he followed the events that led on 14 October 1806 to the defeat of the Prussian army on the ridges east of Weimar, known as the battle of Jena and Auerstedt. However, when French troops threatened him in his own house that same day, he did not know how to react. It was thanks only to Christiane's energetic intervention that his life was spared. He summarised the happenings in his diary: *At five in the evening cannonballs flew through the roofs. At 5.30 arrival of the cavalry. At seven, fires, looting, terrible night.*

Mask of Goethe's face, taken 1807 by Karl Gottlob Weisser for the phrenologist Gall, whose writings on the cranium Goethe had studied. The sculptors Schadow, Rauch and Tieck used this cast in creating busts of Goethe.

Preservation of our house through steadfastness and luck.[205] Two days later an *old resolve* solidified in him: *I wish to recognise as my own, fully and formally, my little friend who has done so much for me and who experienced these hours of trial at my side.*[206] On 19 October he was married to Christiane in the sacristy of the castle church. The approbation which this step found among future generations was not shared by his contemporaries in Weimar. Johanna Schopenhauer, mother of the philosopher, was almost alone in defying a social boycott of Christiane, now Goethe's legal wife.

After the battle of Jena and Auerstedt, Goethe was more than ever convinced of Napoleon's significance. Although previously he had viewed the Corsican primarily as the man who had subdued the French Revolution, he now saw in him the steward of a politically torn continent. He considered a meeting with him in 1808 to be one of the most memorable events of his life. The recognition Napoleon accorded him moved him so deeply that for a long time afterward he spoke of it only in allusions. It was with considerable hesitation that he finally sketched out details of the conversation:

The second [of October]. I am summoned into the chamber. The Emperor is seated at a large round table, breakfasting. To his right, somewhat away from the table, stands Talleyrand; to his left, nearer to him, is Daru, with whom he is talking about war-reparation affairs.

The Emperor nods to me to step forward. I stand at a proper distance in front of him. Having looked at me attentively, he says: Vous êtes un homme.

I bow.

He asks: How old are you?

Sixty years.

You have kept yourself in good trim. – You have written tragedies.

I answered what was necessary. At this point Daru spoke; to flatter the Germans, on whom he had to inflict so much woe, he had become conversant with German letters. He talked about me as perhaps my admir-

ers in Berlin might have; at least I recognised in his words their mode of thought and their attitudes. Daru then added that I had translated from the French, namely Voltaire's Mahomet.

The Emperor interjected: 'It is not a good piece', and he analysed in detail why it was unsuitable for a conqueror of the world to give such an unfavourable account of himself. He then turned the conversation to Werther, which he claimed to have studied thoroughly. After various entirely pertinent observations, he cited a certain passage and said: 'Why did you do that? it isn't natural,' which he explained at great length and quite correctly.

I listened to him with a serene face and responded equably: that I did not know whether anyone else had ever raised the same objection, but that I found it justified and conceded there was something untrue about the passage. However, I added, perhaps the author could be forgiven for having taken a barely noticeable liberty to produce specific effects which he could not have achieved in a simpler, more natural way.

The Emperor stood up, approached me and manoeuvred to cut me off from the other members of the row in which I was standing. Turning his back on them and lowering his voice, he asked whether I was married, whether I had children and other personal matters. I answered unaffectedly. He seemed satisfied and

Napoleon. Small gold-plated bronze figure by an unknown artist. Goethe acquired the statuette for his art collection, where it is still held today. Napoleon received Goethe on 2 October 1808 on the occasion of the Royal Congress in Erfurt. Two further, briefer encounters occurred on 6 and 10 October in Weimar. Retreating from his defeat in Russia, while changing horses in Weimar in December 1812 Napoleon sent greetings to Goethe.

translated my responses into his own terms, only in a somewhat more decisive manner than I had spoken.

I must note the variety of ways in which he expressed his approbation, for he seldom listened without some response, either nodding thoughtfully or saying 'oui' or 'c'est bien' or something similar. Nor should I forget to mention that after he had spoken he usually added: 'Qu'en dit Monsieur Göt?'

When the opportunity presented itself, I inquired of the chamberlain with a gesture whether I should withdraw, to which he replied in the affirmative. I then made my farewells without further ado.[207]

By concentrating on his work, Goethe tried to create a counterweight to the unrest and uncertainties of the time. Lacking the intellectual exchange that his relationship with Schiller had provided, politically isolated as a result of his reserve toward the anti-Napoleonic public and also piqued by the cool reaction in Weimar following his marriage to Christiane, he lived a somewhat secluded life. Along with a variety of activities for the scientific institutes at the university in Jena, he continued his own mineralogical and botanical studies. He drafted a *Metamorphosis of Animals* and worked intensively on his *Theory of Colours*, which eventually became a volume of over a thousand pages. In contrast to the English physicist Isaac Newton, who had advanced the view – confirmed by modern research – that all colours are present in white light, Goethe believed that they originated in cloudiness, resulting from an interplay of light and dark. The reserved responses to the *Theory of Colours* when it was published in 1810 were a disappointment, for he tended to think that his optical studies rather than his literary works constituted his most lasting achievements.

Typical for Goethe's approach is a passage in the *didactic section* of the *Theory of Colours*: *The eye owes its existence to light. From neutral animal auxiliary organs, light calls forth an organ similar to itself; and thus the eye is created by light for light, so that the inner light*

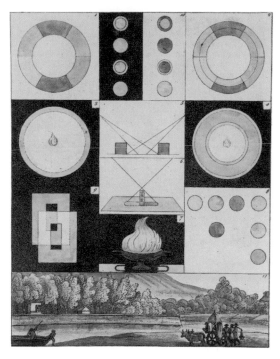

First of the *Plates Accompanying Goethe's Theory of Colours*. The work, which included seven plates, appeared in 1810 as a quarto booklet in an edition of 100 copies. Goethe placed particular importance on the circle of colours that constituted the *First Image* of the plate. In his commentary he characterized this circle of colours as a *completely satisfactory scheme*: yellow, blue and red represent a *triad* that is separated by the *intermediary, mixed or derived* colours – green, purple and orange.

nears the outer. We recall in this connection the old Ionic school of thought, which emphasised that only like can recognise like; and also the ancient mystic's words, which can be expressed thus:

> *Were the eye not like the sun,*
> *How could we behold the light?*
> *If no godly power lived in us,*
> *How could we find in God delight?*

No one will deny the direct relationship between light and eye, but imagining the two to be one and the same is more difficult. It may be easier to grasp if one asserts that the eye has within it a still light that is aroused at the slightest internal or external prompting. In the dark we can call up the brightest images using our power of imagination. In dreams, objects appear to us as if in clear daylight. When awake we notice the slightest beam of external light; indeed, when the eye is struck by accident, light and colours emanate from it.[208]

The insights Goethe achieved in the sciences carried over to his literary work. Thus the process of metamorphosis is a decisive element in all his writings. He considered *polarity*[209] and *enhancement,*[210] key concepts in his thought about nature, to be components of human existence as well. Polarity, the continuous interplay of attracting and repelling, is manifested in the dialogues between Faust and Mephistopheles, and also in the conjunction of light and darkness in the *Theory of Colours*. *Enhancement*, in nature the emergence of new species, finds expression in Goethe's autobiographical writings as growing levels of self-realisation.

Despite the importance that Goethe ascribed to his scientific endeavours, he no longer focused on them as exclusively as in the years after his return from Italy. Between 1806 and 1814, he produced almost more literary works than in the period of his friendship with Schiller. In the spring of 1806, he completed the *First Part* of *Faust*, to which he had been adding since the *Fragment* was published almost 20 years earlier. He also returned to *Wilhelm Meister*. After revising the *Apprenticeship* for a new edition of his works, he began in 1807 to draft the opening chapter of the *Journeyman Years*, with its wealth of stories. He composed *Pandora, a Celebration* that in a time of political uncertainties called attention to the values of beauty, art and science. An encounter with Minchen Herzlieb, the 18-year-old foster daughter of the Jena bookdealer Frommann, found expression in *Sonnets* tinged with resignation, and also in *Elective Affinities*. The novel's ethical rigour, which culminated in a call for the indissolubility of marriage, implying self-consuming renunciation, led to passionate discussions among the reading public, an interest which has been maintained even into the 21st century.

After completing the historical section of the *Theory of Colours*, as well as a biography of Philipp Hackert, the painter, whose personal papers he had inherited, Goethe at last resolved to write about his own life. *I had reason to ask why I did not undertake for myself what I had done for someone else? Thus even before finishing the [Hackert] piece I turned to the story of my own earliest years. Here I found that I had hesitated too long. I should have begun the work while my mother was still alive. Then I would have been closer in years to those childhood scenes and would have been transported there through her keen gift of memory. Now, however, I had to call forth these vanished spirits from within myself, laboriously gathering together many an aid to memory, like a conjurer assembling his tools. I had to portray the development of a child who later became prominent, and the particular circumstances under which this occurred, but also how this is relevant for the insightful observer of human nature. To this effect I called my memoirs modestly enough: Truth and Poetry, deeply convinced that in the present, but even more in memory, one models the world according to one's own nature.*[211]

After such intensive preparation, in 1811 Goethe began dictating the work, whose title he then amended to the more euphonious *Poetry and Truth* [Dichtung und Wahrheit]. A year later, he completed the first two parts; the third, which encompassed the events surrounding the genesis of *Werther*, followed in 1813. Soon thereafter, inspired by the work of the Persian poet Hafiz, who almost half a millennium earlier had celebrated nature and love despite political turbulence, he conceived a lengthy cycle of poems. Following Hafiz's example, he intended to publish it under the title *Divan*, Persian for 'collection'.

The years after Schiller's death saw the beginning of Goethe's regular visits to spas in Bohemia. Sometimes he withdrew for almost two months to Carlsbad, Teplitz or Marienbad. Along with taking the waters, which he credited with having a beneficial effect on his health, his stays were governed by writing and research. He dictated considerable portions of his publications there. At the same time he enjoyed the stimulus afforded him by the spa's relaxed company. In addition to Zelter, Duke Carl August and Wilhelm von Humboldt, he was close to the diplomat Karl Friedrich von Reinhard and to Joseph Sebastian Grüner, a municipal councillor from the nearby town of Eger. He also encountered Empress Maria Ludovica of Austria and Louis

Marienbad with Pump House. Chalk drawing with colour wash by Goethe, after 1820. Between 1785 and 1823, Goethe paid 17 visits to spas in Bohemia, especially to Carlsbad and Marienbad.

Bonaparte, brother of Napoleon. A mutual interest in the natural sciences brought him together with the mineralogist Gottlob Werner and the Swedish chemist Berzelius.

Goethe's position during the Napoleonic years was characterised by an increasing reserve toward the Romantics, with literature now assuming a more important place in his concerns than the visual arts. He could muster little understanding for the Romantic tendency to fantasy and hyperbole, which he felt easily led to the *bizarre, grotesque and ridiculous*.[212] Even his cordial contacts with individual authors, and the esteem in which they held him, did little to alter his growing aloofness. Mindful of his own efforts in Strasbourg, he welcomed with an approving review *Des Knaben Wunderhorn*, a collection of folk songs compiled by Clemens Brentano and Achim von Arnim, but remained cool to the editors' own productions. When Kleist, using the biblical supplication 'on the knees of my heart',[213] sent him the fragment *Penthesilea* in 1808, he responded guardedly. Out of personal dislike he distanced himself from the Schlegel brothers: *Unhappy persons their whole life long, they want to be more than nature has granted them*.[214] With Philipp Otto Runge he shared similar views on the essence of colours, but he rejected the painting *The Times of Day* and similar works: *Whoever stands at the brink like this must either perish or go mad; there is no mercy*.[215] Almost alone Goethe's relationship with Schelling, whose philosophy of nature he referred to in the *Second Part* of *Faust*, remained untroubled. Bettina Brentano, whom he knew as the granddaughter of Sophie von La Roche and protégée of his own mother, and to whose enthusiastic admiration he was not averse, caused a break with him due to her impertinences toward Christiane.

An encounter with Beethoven in the summer of 1812 demonstrated how Goethe tended to retreat behind a *hard shell*[216] to protect his mental equilibrium. After learning that Beethoven was creating music to *Egmont*, he had expressed the hope of one day being able to *enjoy his extraordinary talent*[217] in person. But when Beethoven indeed played *delightfully*[218] for him at Teplitz, he could not reciprocate the composer's respectful admiration: *His talent amazed me; but alas he is a totally unrestrained individual, who may not be wrong to find the world detestable, but in doing so certainly does not make it more enjoyable either for himself or for others.*[219]

Citizen of the World

At times after Schiller's death it seemed to Goethe as if he, too, were nearing the end of his existence. Yet a journey to the Rhine and Main area in the summer of 1814, after the *political skies*[220] had cleared, was a *rejuvenating experience*.[221] Seeing his native region again, a *salutary cure* at the spa in Wiesbaden and the *sympathy of astute and loving friends,* all converged to effect *a revival and intensification of a state of happiness*[222]. In Frankfurt, the wife of banker Johann Jakob von Willemer, Marianne, whose affection Goethe reciprocated, awakened his ability, almost silenced since the *Roman Elegies*, to speak in poetry *from the fullness of his heart*[223]. The *West-Eastern Divan*, which he had begun already, received an unexpected impetus. When he returned to Frankfurt the following year, spending several weeks at the Willemers' estate on the banks of the Main River, the mysterious

Marianne von Willemer. Chalk drawing by Anton Radl, 1819.
Like Goethe, Marianne von Willemer considered the circumstances of their friendship to be deeply personal. Not until 1849, when she was 64 and long a widow, did she indicate to Herman Grimm (whose father and uncle had compiled *Grimms' Fairy Tales*) that some of the poems in the *West-Eastern Divan* were from her pen, composed as responses to Goethe's poetically-veiled avowals. Grimm, for his part, made these revelations public only in 1869, after Marianne's death.

dialogue of the *Book of Suleika*[224] came into being, in which Marianne von Willemer appears as the lover of his Persian mentor Hafiz. Over the next few years Goethe added a multitude of verses and epigrams to the *Divan*. Western and eastern religion, the poetic calling and perception of nature, human wisdom and human folly, insight into the transitoriness of life but also joy in earthly matters were the themes. Typical of such thoughts, the poem entitled *Blessed Longing* alludes to the law of metamorphosis in human existence:

> *Tell it only to the wise,*
> *For the crowd at once will jeer:*
> *That which is alive I praise,*
> *That which longs for death by fire.*
>
> *Cooled by passionate love at night,*
> *Procreated, procreating,*
> *You have known the alien feeling*
> *In the calm of candlelight;*
>
> *Gloom-embraced will lie no more,*
> *By the flickering shades obscured,*
> *But are seized by new desire,*
> *To a higher union lured.*
>
> *Then no distance holds you fast;*
> *Winged, enchanted, on you fly,*
> *Light your longing, and at last,*
> *Moth, you meet the flame and die.*
>
> *Never prompted to that quest:*
> *Die and dare rebirth!*
> *You remain a dreary guest*
> *On our gloomy earth.*[225]

Several visits Goethe paid to the brothers Sulpiz and Melchior Boisserée in Heidelberg were consequential for him. Their collection of medieval paintings from secularized monasteries and churches along the Lower Rhine was like a revelation. Indeed, the richness of what he saw threatened to overwhelm him. Genuinely moved by Rogier van der Weyden's *Altar of the Three Wise Men*, he confessed: *In order to survive in old age, one tries to maintain equilibrium by avoiding notions of a new and disturbing nature – but now a previously unknown world of colours and objects has burst forth, forcing me out of the rut of my opinions.*[226] The authenticity of this statement, recorded by a confidante of the Boisserées, can scarcely be doubted. And yet, it was valid only in a relative sense. Goethe, who was not only immersed in the world of Hafiz, but also revising his *Italian Journey* and continuing his scientific studies, could ultimately do no more than regard medieval painting with sincere interest and accord it a place in his total concept of the world of art. Nonetheless, his reserve toward anything that was not classical had been breached, and his relationship with the Boiserées continued after their first meeting.

Following his stay in Wiesbaden and Frankfurt Goethe travelled north to the Rhine province, decreed Prussian by the Congress of Vienna. At the request of Minister of State vom Stein, his host, he drew up a memorandum on *Art and Antiquity along the Rhine and Main*. In it he not only gave an account of existing structures, collections

Contemporary Events, 1815–1833

1815 Holy Alliance of Austria, Russia and Prussia

1817 Student societies protest at the Wartburg calling for more liberal rule by German states

1819 Carlsbad Resolution Decrees aimed at supressing student protests

1821–1829 Greek struggle for independence from Turkish domination

1830 July Revolution in Paris. Unrest in central Germany

1832 Demonstrations in Hambach urging democratic rule in Germany

1833 Establishment of a German Customs Union

and academic institutes, but tried to encourage *activity on the part of all those concerned.*[227] He advocated efforts to resume construction on the Cologne cathedral, suspended for centuries. In addition to offering recommendations for the preservation of specific artifacts, he proposed improving the level of education in Germany. He felt that the closed universities in Cologne and Bonn should be given a fresh start: *In our days we should no longer talk about schools or factions of scholarship but about views common to all, based on real knowledge.*[228] The piece on the Rhineland's art institutions later grew into the journal *On Art and Antiquity.*

Although he experienced his visits to the Rhine and Main regions as a form of *rebirth,*[229] the following years again brought Goethe pain and disappointment. On 6 June 1816, Christiane died. In his diary, where his dictated notes were usually factual

Goethe in his study, dictating to his copyist Johann August John. Oil painting by Joseph Schmeller, 1831.

and impersonal, he could not conceal his emotion: *My wife nearing her end. Final frightful struggle of her being. She departed toward midday. Emptiness and deathly quiet in and around me.*[230] When in the same summer, at the start of a third trip to southern Germany, an axle on his coach broke shortly beyond Weimar, he regarded the accident as a warning from Providence and decided no longer to undertake extensive journeys. Finally, intrigues spun by the actress Caroline Jagemann, a favourite of Grand Duke Carl August, led Goethe to resign in April 1817 from the directorship of the Weimar theatre. Not unjustly, he was

Goethe's method of dictating was described by his secretary Johann Christian Schuchardt: 'In the last eight years of his life I never saw him do more at the writing stand than sign his name; his practice was to dictate. He did not pace back and forth as he spoke, for the room was too small; instead, he walked around the table. Words flowed from his mouth without stop, so that I was scarcely able to follow with my pen. He had thoroughly worked out his formulations in advance. He appeared not to notice his surroundings; if he was interrupted or called to greet a visitor, on returning he had not lost his train of thought, but resumed dictation without even asking to hear the sentence at which he had left off.'

affronted by the manner in which he was let go after his 40-year association with the activities there, and he remained irritated with the Grand Duke for some time.

Viewed as a whole, Goethe's last two decades were marked less by external events than by regular work, progressing from day to day. Increasingly, the austere *back room*[231] of his house – with an adjoining library and a small bedroom – became the centre of his existence. In the low-ceilinged chamber facing the rear gardens, detached from the outer world, he could conduct morphological experiments, read and dictate. The extent of what he achieved is almost incomprehensible. Along with supervising the Duchy's institutes of science and art, for which he remained responsible to the end of his life, his own production was enormous. The works on which he concentrated after the *West-Eastern Divan*, mainly *Wilhelm Meister's Journeyman Years* and the *Second Part* of *Faust*, became repositories of his legacy to the future. In addition, he continued the retrospective description of his own life: in 1816 he completed the *First Part* of his *Italian Journey*, in 1822 the *Campaign in France*, in 1829 the *Second Sojourn in Rome*. Two journals that he had edited since 1816, *On Art and Antiquity* and *On the Sciences in General*, gave him an opportunity to communicate with knowledgeable counterparts outside of Weimar. Because the journals included personally-tinged reviews, as well as reports about acquisitions for his collections, they reflect the scope of his many interests, also his likes and dislikes.

Along with the literary and editorial activities that brought him into contact with the outside world, he exchanged letters with a large number of contemporaries. In addition to his correspondence with Zelter, in which he noted many thoughts on the arts as well as on human affairs, his letters to Reinhard, to Sulpiz Boisserée and to Wilhelm von Humboldt are significant. They became more condensed than in earlier years, typified by locutions that could be characterised as 'glimpses of higher things'. Thus he greeted Zelter with the words *May the moral order of the world sustain you*,[232] and he closed a letter to Boisserée with *Commending the most devoted and loyal to the wellspring of everything beautiful and good*.[233] Individually, such symbol-laden phrases – which appear hundreds of times as a greeting, a reminiscence or a hint of something to come – seem to be isolated comments. Considered in their entirety, however, they convey the impression that Goethe formulated them with a purpose, indeed that he intended them to be messages to posterity.

A key to understanding Goethe's many-faceted activity can be seen in his attempts to utilise every moment. *Time is endlessly long, and each day a vessel into which much can be poured if one really wants to fill it,*[234] he remarked in *Poetry and Truth*. How he tried to accomplish his projects by heeding every hour is revealed by the diaries he kept for 52 years, and with absolute regularity after 1806. The entries helped him to live in the moment but also to distance himself from it; they allowed him to view a single event as a part of the course of his life, recognising *the past in the present.*[235] Nothing better illustrates his assertion that his existence was little more than effort and toil, seeming to him as if he were *eternally lifting a rock that always had to be heaved anew,*[236] than do his daily notes.

Despite continuing to focus on his work, Goethe no longer tended to withdraw from his surroundings as he had done in earlier years. He welcomed guests almost daily, often to a display of his

Goethe's house at the Frauenplan in Weimar. Engraving by Ludwig Schütze with a facsimile of Goethe's words and signature from 1828:

Why are they standing out there?   *If they would just come inside,*
Isn't there a door, and a gate?   *They would be well received.*

Goethe first rented the house in 1782. Ten years later he received the deed to it as a gift from Duke Carl August. He lived there until his death.

collections or to a chamber concert. The less he left Weimar, the more he opened his house to the world. Typically, most of his visitors were not writers and poets but scientists and scholars of art, explorers and educators, men and women of practical experience.

Goethe's hospitality had its limits, however. To protect himself from people who considered him a local attraction, he could be intentionally rude. This gave rise to the rumour that he was a magisterial old man who encountered those unknown to him from an almost unbridgeable distance. The Bavarian historian Karl Heinrich von Lang reported in 1826: 'On my journey I stopped in Weimar, where, dazzled by the devil, I sent a note that spared no subservient obeisances to the city's old Faust, Mister von Goethe, in hopes of meeting with him. I was received at half past noon. A tall, old, ice-cool, stiff, imperial councillor came toward me in a dressing gown, gestured to me to seat myself, accepted everything I told him about the aspirations of the King of Bavaria and then barked: *Tell me, no doubt you have a fire insurance office in your Ansbach region?* Answer: Yes, indeed. – Then came the invitation to recount to the last detail the procedures that were followed when fires occurred. I responded to him that it depended whether the fire could be extinguished or the town or house actually burnt. – *Let us, if I may say so, permit the town to go up in flames.* – And so I fanned my blaze and let it consume everything, with the fire engines rushing around in vain; set out on my inspection the next day, obtained an estimate of the damages and pared it down as much as possible; made some superficial sketches of the buildings that will remain neglected by the Munich supervisors, while the poor burnt-out inhabitants languish in shanties; and finally in two, three years paid out the compensation sums after they had been reduced to almost nothing. The old Faust listened to this and said: *I thank you.* Then he continued: *What is the population of such a district in your area?* I said: Something over 500,000 souls. – *So! So!* he intoned. *Hm! Hm! That is indeed something.* (To be sure, more than twice the entire Grand Duchy of Weimar.) I said: Now, as I have the honour of being here with you, there is one soul less. However, I shall get myself hence, and take leave of you. – Whereupon he gave me his hand, thanked me for the honour of my visit and accompanied me to the door. I felt as if I had caught a cold while putting out fires.'[237]

Independent of the stream of guests, a small group of friends and close associates surrounded Goethe. Along with Zelter, Meyer and Chancellor von Müller, the Grand Duchy's chief judicial officer, he put his trust in the physician Karl Vogel, the philologist Friedrich Wilhelm Riemer and Frédéric Soret, a scientist who had come to Weimar from Geneva to tutor Carl August's grandchildren. In 1823 this circle was joined by Johann Peter Eckermann, a 30-year-old autodidact and enthusiastic admirer of Goethe's works. Over the next decade, he became an almost indispensable assistant, primarily in editorial and archival activities. His published *Conversations with Goethe* were considered by as demanding a reader as Nietzsche to be among the most important works ever written in the German language.

Goethe's innermost circle was made up of his family. His son August, to whom he was deeply attached, entered the Duchy's civil service after studying law, and became his father's assistant in the supervision of artistic and scientific institutions. A year after Christiane's death, August married Ottilie von Pogwisch, daughter of a Prussian officer

August von Goethe. Chalk drawing by Joseph Schmeller, around 1823.
To gain distance from professional and domestic problems, on his father's advice August undertook an extended trip to Italy. He contracted smallpox there and died on 27 October 1830 in Rome.

and a lady-in-waiting at the Weimar court. She brought much conviviality to Goethe's house but also a certain unrest, due to her volatility. Over time her marriage to August became difficult, burdening him scarcely less than did working in the shadow of his patriarchical father. Three children, Walther, Wolfgang and Alma, were born to August and Ottilie in 1818, 1820 and 1827. Goethe was a solicitous grandfather who let the children play in his presence and took an interest in their education. With the boys he sometimes perceived *pedagogical problems*,[238] but he seems in general to have been patient with them, even forgetting his stinginess with time when they were around.

A profound turning-point in Goethe's later years occurred during his final journey to a Bohemian spa in 1823. His unflagging ability and readiness to devote himself to another person led him to experience one more *passionate state*.[239] A fatherly affection for Ulrike von Levetzow, granddaughter of his host in Marienbad, developed into an almost youthful love. At 74 he went so far as to woo the 19-year-old. Concerns on the part of her family, and not least Ulrike's own reluctance, moved him to relinquish the courtship. He sensed that this would be the last *blissful height*[240] of his life. It found expression in the *Marienbad Elegy*, delicately making a connection between his personal *wishing, hoping and desiring*[241] and his belief in man's godlike qualities:

Ulrike von Levetzow as a 17-year-old, two years before Goethe courted her in Marienbad. Pastel portrait by an unknown artist, 1821.

The power to love was gone, all gone the needing
Of love's response outflowing from another;
Then hopes, bright plans, resolve, the deed succeeding,
Again the zest of living I discover!
If ever love was lover's inspiration
It gave in me a lovely demonstration.

And all through her! – A fearful indecision
Oppressed the mind and body, all frustrated:
Grim spectres all around the prisoned vision
In anxious heartvoid's wasteland desolated;
The threshold now with gleams of hope is clearing
As she in gentle sunshine is appearing.

The peace of God, more happiness bestowing
Than all our understanding – scripture tells us –
Can be compared with peace that comes from knowing
The loved one's presence that serenely quells us;
The heart's at rest, nought mars the deep, deep feeling
That we belong to her for life and healing.

Towards a Higher, Purer, Unknown driven
We sense our purity of heart inclining
In grateful self-surrender freely given,
The Evernameless-One thereby divining;
We call this: reverence! – Just so I adore her
And it is ecstasy to stand before her.[242]

The renunciation of personal passion expressed in the *Marienbad Elegy* and, linked to it, the irrevocable feeling of being old, the impending completion of his autobiography and the deaths of contemporaries, caused Goethe to turn his gaze to the *lasting and* the lost[243] of his existence. *If I may confide in you, as I have done before,* he wrote to Wilhelm von Humboldt in 1831, *I admit that at my advanced age everything appears increasingly historical: whether an event occurred in the past, in a distant land or spatially and temporally close to me is one and the same; indeed, I seem myself to have become more and more a part of history.*[244] Similarly, Goethe felt how much his intellectual endeavours were influenced by his environment. He called himself a *collective being*[245] who was continuously receptive and learning: *It is true, in my long life I have done and created a good number of things of which I could be proud. Nonetheless, what did I have that was truly my own other than the capability and the inclination to see and to hear, to differentiate and to choose, and to enliven the seen and the heard with some spirit and give an account of it with some skill?*[246]

The more his own existence seemed to him to recede, the more Goethe reflected on future developments in the world as he knew it. Anticipating the growth of journalism in coming decades, he spoke of *these dreadful times of a niggling and divisive press,*[247] which brings *a sort of semi-culture* to the masses, but for the productive talent is *a poison that destroys the tree of creative ability.*[248] In *Wilhelm Meister's Journeyman Years* he discussed the dangers of the *spread of machines*, which *like a thunderstorm are slowly, slowly* surging forward, which will *come and strike.*[249] And in a letter to Zelter he complained about the restlessness of the younger generation: *Everything nowadays is ultra; everything transcends, in thought and in deeds. No one knows himself any more, no one understands the element in which he moves and acts, no one the material with which he is working. Young people get stirred up much too early, and then are carried away by the whirlpool of the times. Wealth and speed are what the world admires, and are aspired to by all. Railways, mail-coaches, steamships and all possible means of communication – those in the civilized world try to outdo each other in producing these things, thereby only to persist in mediocrity.*[250]

Although with such observations Goethe located himself among the *last of an era that will not soon recur,*[251] at times he regretted that he would not witness the advances of the century. On learning of a suggestion by Alexander von Humboldt that a canal be dredged through the Isthmus of Panama, he spoke of the prospects for world shipping that would result: *Should a dig of this sort succeed, so that ships of any size, with any cargo, could sail from the Gulf of Mexico to the Pacific Ocean, the consequences for the human race, civilized and uncivilized, would be incalculable. I should be surprised, however, if the United States missed taking this project into its hands. One can expect that this youthful nation, with its westward drive, will in 30 to 40 years have occupied and populated the vast lands beyond the Rocky Mountains . . . Secondly, I should like to see a connection forged between the Rhine and the Danube. But this undertaking would be so gigantic that I doubt it can be achieved, especially in view of our German resources . . . And finally, I should like to see the English in possession of a canal at Suez. I wish I might live to experience these three achievements – it would be worth lasting some 50 more years.*[252] Goethe set these thoughts down in 1827. The Suez Canal was completed in 1869, the Panama Canal in 1914. A connection between the Danube and the Rhine rivers came into being only in the late 20th century.

Goethe's interest in world affairs corresponded to his literary concerns. Familiar in his youth with significant works not only by German but also French and English authors, and having pondered about classical antiquity during his friendship with Schiller, he had since explored the world of the Orient in working on his *Divan* and, at the urging of the Boiserées, had *feasted at the table of the Nibelungs.*[253] Now he made a systematic attempt to gain an overview of the letters of other nations, including India and China. Almost obsessively he read upcoming authors such as Byron, Walter Scott, Mérimée, Victor Hugo and Manzoni. In his journal *On Art and Antiquity* he suggested emphatically that literature is *a common good of mankind*, created everywhere and in every age *by hundreds and hundreds of people.*[254] He ultimately conceived the idea of a process of interchange among representatives of various

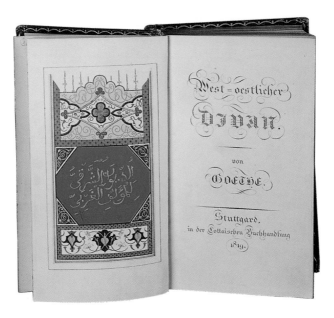

Coloured frontispiece and title page of the *West-Eastern Divan*. The Arabic inscription reads: *The Eastern Divan by a Western author.*

national literatures and proposed calling it *world literature*. To this effect he asserted in a memorandum of March 1830: *If such a world literature should take shape in the near future, as will be inevitable with the continually increasing speed of communication, we may expect of it nothing more and nothing less than what it can accomplish and does indeed accomplish. The wide world, as large as it is, is still only an extended homeland and strictly speaking will give us no more than what our native soil also brought forth . . . Certainly there are people every-where who care about what has been established and hence are concerned about the true progress of mankind.* [255]

Translations were for Goethe a crucial means of forging connections among different cultures. He promoted not only the Schlegel brothers' adaptations of Shakespeare but also the efforts of others, such as the Berlin scholar Johann Diederich Gries, who rendered the writings of Calderón and Dante into German. And his own efforts were not inconsiderable: from the Italian he translated Benvenuto Cellini's *Vita*; from the French, *Rameau's Nephew* by Diderot and Voltaire's tragedy *Mahomet*. In addition, he rendered into German numerous poems from the Spanish, Croatian, Finnish and modern Greek.

Paralleling his thoughts on the universality of literature, Goethe's religious convictions became more general, as well. Although in his youth he had situated himself somewhere between a poetically veiled pantheism and a *Christianity for my personal use*,[256] and in his early years in Weimar had professed an ethical humanism, in his later years he believed increasingly that *because of the diverse elements of his mind* he could *not be satisfied with only one way of thinking.*[257] Deliberately apodictic, he wrote to Jacobi in 1813: *As a writer and an artist I am a polytheist, but a pantheist as a natural scientist, and each one as resolutely as the other. If I have need of a God for myself as a civilized human being, that is also provided for. The things of heaven and earth constitute a realm so vast that the faculties of all beings combined can only begin to comprehend it.*[258]

Just as at the age of 24 in the *Letter of the Pastor* he had criticized the Church's presentation of Christ's teachings, in his later years Goethe rejected tenets that were narrowly dogmatic or congealed in orthodoxy. When his earlier pen-friend Auguste zu Stolberg, later wife of the Danish government minister Bernstorff,

In Goethe the outstanding features of German genius come together. He possesses all of them to a high degree, having a great depth of thought, as well as a grace that originates in imaginative powers and is considerably rarer than the charm acquired in social intercourse. He also has an at times fanciful excitability and a versatility, which attract readers who desire something that will enliven their monotonous existence and who demand that the fictional take the place of real events for them.

Germaine de Staël,
De l'Allemagne, 1813

made a touching attempt to 'save'[259] him, he retreated behind noncommittal remarks: *To live a long time means to outlive quite a lot: beloved, hated, indifferent individuals, kingdoms, capital cities, even forests and trees that we sowed and planted in our youth. We take pleasure in all these transitory things; if we never lose sight of the eternal, we shan't suffer from the passage of time. My whole life long I have tried to be honest with myself and others, and in all my earthly doings I have always had the highest goals; you and yours have done so, as well. Thus let us continue to carry out our duties; so long as it is day for us, the sun will shine for others, too; they will distinguish themselves and inspire us. Let us not worry about the future! In our Father's kingdom are many mansions, and as He has prepared such a happy place for us on earth, both of us will surely be taken care of on the other side.*[260]

With reservations about ecclesiastical institutions but full of respect for the *dignity and ethical culture of Christianity as it shimmers and lights the way for us in the Gospels,*[261] Goethe expressed hope that humanity would succeed in finding its way *gradually from a Christianity of word and creed increasingly to a Christianity of attitude and deed.*[262] In this spirit of non-sectarian piety he tended to espouse a universalism, of which one finds indications in the *Second Part* of *Faust*, in *Wilhelm Meister's Journeyman Years* and in his late lyrics. Along with *Proemion*, *One and All*, and *Orphic Words*, the poem entitled *Testament*, written in 1829, can be considered part of a cycle of lyrical confessions:

> *No thing on earth to nought can fall,*
> *The Eternal onward moves in all;*
> *Rejoice, by being be sustained.*
> *Being is deathless: living wealth,*
> *With which the All adorns itself,*
> *By laws abides and is maintained.*

Long since, the true was found and could
Spirits join in brotherhood;
The ancient truth set hand upon.
Thank now the sage, O child of earth,
Who showed her and her kin the path
For circuiting about the sun.

Now turn yourself about, within:
Your centre you will find therein,
No noble soul can this gainsay.
No principle within you'll miss,
For independent conscience is
The sun that rules your moral day.

The senses next you must believe;
With nothing false will they deceive
If intellect keeps you awake.
Be fresh of eye, with joy attend;
A way, footsure and supple, wend,
A walk in worlds of pasture take.

Be moderate when blessings flow,
Good sense in every detail show
Where life is in its ecstasies;
Then bygone time gives permanence,
The future lives, and in advance:
Eternity the moment is. [263]

Goethe hesitated to speak in the form of a direct confession. All the more significant, therefore, is a personal statement he made to Sulpiz Boisserée on 22 March 1831, a year to the day before his own death, adding it as a postscript to a long letter: *On this last page I cannot resist the temptation to close with something odd, both in earnest and in jest. No human being can resist religious feeling, but it is impossible for him to process it alone, and thus he seeks or creates fellow-believers. The latter is not my nature, but the former I have performed faithfully, and, beginning with the Story of Creation, I have found no creed that I could embrace fully. Now in my old age I learn of a sect in Asia Minor, the Hypsistarians, who, surrounded by heathens, Jews and Christians, decided they would treasure, admire and honour the best, the most perfect things that might come to their attention, and if something*

Goethe at the age of 68. Coloured engraving by Johann Müller after a chalk drawing by the Weimar court painter Ferdinand Jagemann.

appeared to have a close relationship to God they would even worship it. Suddenly in a dark age I noticed a cheerful light, for I felt all my life I had been aspiring to qualify as an Hypsistarian. But that is no small task: for how does one, within the limitations of one's individuality, gain knowledge of the most excellent?[264]

Neither his constant activities nor his wide-ranging correspondence and social contacts could blind Goethe to the fact that age and attitudes increasingly separated him from succeeding generations. Solitary, *like Merlin from his shining grave*, he sometimes felt he could hear *his own echo.*[265] In 1827 he wrote to Zelter: *The circle of people closest to me seems to be like a cluster of sibylline leaves, which are consumed one after the other by the flames of life and dispersed into the air, thus from moment to moment making more precious those who remain.*[266]

Severest ordeals[267] confronted Goethe with the death of Grand Duke Carl August in 1828 and with the *departure*[268] of his son two years later. After *caring friends*[269] brought him the news of August's death in Rome, he shrouded himself in silence. *With force*[270] he immersed himself in work that was still unfinished, particularly the final chapters of *Poetry and Truth* and the *Second Part* of *Faust*, and tried to become *totally absorbed*[271] by them. Out of concern for August's family, he drew up his will and arranged for the posthumous printing of his works. *Only the great concept of duty*, it seemed to him at the time, could sustain him. *I have no care but to keep myself in physical equilibrium; everything else will follow in turn. The body must, the mind will, and he who finds the most necessary path stipulated need not worry too much.*[272]

In order to escape a *quite overdone celebration*[273] of his 82nd birthday, Goethe left Weimar for the last time in August 1831 to spend a few days at Ilmenau in the Thuringian Forest. From there he made an excursion to the village of Gabelbach and to the hunting lodge on top of the Kickelhahn where he had stayed numerous times before. Mine inspector Johann Mahr, the only person who

What makes time speed by?
  Activity!
What makes it unbearably long?
  Idleness!
What causes you to incur debt?
  Lingering and suffering!
What helps you to win?
  Not hesitating too long!
What brings you honour?
  Defending yourself!

accompanied him, provided a simple record of the visit: 'We ascended quite comfortably to the highest point of the Kickelhahn, where he stepped out and delighted in the splendid view of the hills, and then exclaimed: *Oh, if only my good Grand Duke Carl August could have seen this beautiful view once more!* – Then he requested: *That small house in the woods must be nearby. I can go there by myself, and the chaise should wait here until we return.* And in fact, he strode vigorously through the blueberry bushes that grew rather high on the crest of the mountain onward to the two-storey lodge built out of logs. A steep flight of steps leads to the upper level; I offered to help him up, but even though his eighty-second birthday was the next day, he declined with youthful cheerfulness, saying: *Don't think I cannot climb the stairs; I can still manage quite well.* Upon entering the room he noted: *Long ago I spent eight summer days in this chamber with my servant, and at that time I wrote a little verse on the wall. I should like to see this verse again, and if there is a mention of the day on which it was written, be so good as to note it down for me.* I led him to the room's southern window, to the left of which was written in pencil:

O'er all the hill-tops
Is quiet now,
In all the tree-tops
Hearest thou
Hardly a breath;
The birds are asleep in the trees:
Wait, soon like these
Thou, too, shalt rest. 7 September 1780

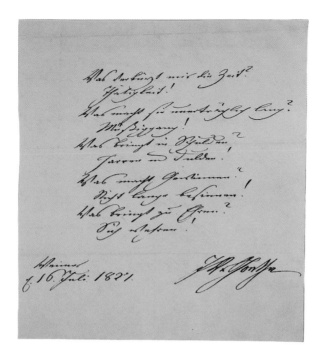

An epigram from the *Book of Observations* in the *West-Eastern Divan*, in Goethe's hand. A translation of the text is given in the sidebar on the facing page.

Goethe read these few lines, and tears flowed down his cheeks. Very slowly he drew a snow-white handkerchief from his dark brown coat, dried his tears and spoke in a gentle, melancholy tone: *Yes, wait, soon thou, too, shalt rest!* He was silent for half a minute, looked once more through the window over the darkening spruces and turned to me with the words: *Now let us go back.*'[274]

Faust

Generally considered the most significant poetic work written in German, Goethe's drama *Faust* was the product of a long evolution. Not only did Goethe labour over it almost his entire life, a number of pens before his had dealt with the story, over a span of three centuries. Basically, all Faust tales can be traced to a man of the 16th century about whom contemporaries spoke with a mixture of fear and awe. Extensive research has shown that Jörg or Johannes Faust was probably born around 1480 in the town of Knittlingen, in southwestern Germany. By the time he was 30, he appears to have been known as an astrologer, also as a quack and a braggart. Gossip about him spread, due to the willingness of the uneducated to believe in marvels. But the accounts gave evidence, too, of an individualistic way of thinking that came to characterize the age of the Renaissance and the Reformation. Reports that Faust had achieved miraculous results in alchemy, and that he was interested in the sciences, which were now becoming increasingly divorced from theology, found open ears. As early as 1570, a Latin manuscript recounting his feats circulated among students at the progressive university of Wittenberg. Not much later, in 1587, a chapbook dealing with the subject, the *Historie of Doctor Johann Faustus, the Famous Sorcerer and Practitioner of Black Magic*, appeared in print. Advancing the not fully convincing justification that his book demonstrated the dangers of audacious iniquity, the anonymous author compiled stories already in circulation and added new ones to them. A decisive feature was now that the devil appeared in the form of Mephistopheles, with whom Faust signed a mysterious pact.

Before the 16th century came to an end, the legend, by then widespread in Germany, made its way to England, where Christopher Marlowe, Shakespeare's contemporary, created a stirring tragedy out of the episodes previously just loosely linked. For the first time the man who signed a pact with the devil was portrayed as a rebel against the might of God, craving supernatural knowledge and worldly power. Through performances by itinerant actors, this rendition returned to the Continent, thrilling people even more than did the chapbooks that continued to appear in ever new versions. Having adopted stage effects from courtly operas and incorporated a harlequin figure who as Faust's merry servant threatened to outshine his master, the story developed further during the Baroque era, but it lost inner power. With the advent of the Enlightenment, the once so impressive play sank to the level of puppet stages. Lessing tried to create a bourgeois tragedy out of the subject, but completed only a few scenes, finding it difficult to transform the demonic magus into a man of reason. Not until the Storm and Stress period did authors in Germany take up the tale again: Klinger, Maler Müller and eventually Goethe.

By his own account, Goethe had drafted a plan for a Faust drama as early as his time in Strasbourg. Although it is unclear what his concept was then, we do know that individual scenes, such as the invocation of the Earth Spirit, Mephistopheles advising a student, *Auerbach's Cellar* and parts of the Gretchen tragedy, were composed in Frankfurt between 1773 and 1775. They bear the unmistakable stamp of the literary richness of that time. During his first years in Weimar, Goethe occasionally recited from this version, later identified as *Urfaust*. In Italy he penned some scenes, including the *Witches' Kitchen* and Faust's monologue in the *Forest and Cave*, but increasingly he felt that he would never

Faust. A Fragment. Title page of the first edition. In 1789 Goethe gave the text, which included all the scenes that he was then prepared to publish, to the Leipzig bookdealer Göschen to be printed.

The last page of *Faust. A Fragment.* In the *Cathedral* scene, Gretchen's conscience imagines the presence of an 'evil spirit' during the funeral mass for her mother. At the chorus' appeal to the Last Judgement, *Quid sum miser tunc dicturus* [What should I, miserable person, say then], Gretchen begs her neighbour for her flask of smelling salts, then faints.

finish the piece. Thus in 1789 he decided to allow the existing scenes to be printed in an edition of his collected writings as *Faust. A Fragment.*

It was Schiller who persuaded Goethe to take up his previous plans again. Only a few months after their memorable conversation in Jena, he asked Goethe to let him know more about the still unpublished parts: 'I confess that what I have read so far is the torso of Hercules. A power and an immensity of genius, revealing the highest master, rule these scenes, and I would like to follow the grand and bold soul that breathes in them as far as possible.'[275]

But Goethe still did not muster up the courage *to untie the package that keeps Faust captive.*[276] Not until June 1797 did he respond to Schiller's urging: *As it is imperative that I give myself something to do in my current state of unrest, I have decided to return to Faust, and even if I don't complete it, I shall at least bring it a bit further by separating out what has been printed and arranging what is already written or contemplated into large blocks, thus preparing the execution of the plan, which basically is still only a design. Now I wish, however, that you would be so kind as to think through the matter during a sleepless night and let me know the demands you would make of the whole, thus like a true prophet recounting to me my own dreams and interpreting them.*[277]

Shortly after this letter, Goethe composed the *Dedication* and the *Prelude on the Stage*, and in the years of his exchanges with Schiller did not lose sight of the piece. In the spring of 1806 he managed to fill in the last remaining gaps in *Part I*.

Although the title and contents of the tragedy, printed in 1808, hint at a second part, Goethe wrote nothing more on *Faust* for 20 years. That he resumed work on it was due not least to Eckermann. As had Schiller with *Part I*, Eckermann kept prodding Goethe, until in February 1825 he returned to the manuscripts that had lain idle. Writing on the drama became his *main business*[278] for the next six years. In a letter to Heinrich Meyer of July 1831 he reminisced: *I knew for a long time what, indeed even how, I wanted it to be and for many years carried it around with me like a private fairy tale, executing from time to time only such scenes as appealed to me. The second part should not and could not be as fragmentary as the first. Reason has more of a voice there, as one will indeed have seen from the texts that have been printed. To be sure, it finally required a forceful decision to pull the whole thing together, so that it could stand up to the scrutiny of educated minds. I was determined that it should be completed before my birthday. And so it shall be. The entire play lies before me, and I have only minor*

The Earth Spirit appears before Faust. Pencil drawing by Goethe, 1810–1812.

details still to correct. In this form I shall seal it up, and then it may add to the value of my posthumous volumes. If it contains enough problems – as do the history of the world and humanity – in that the problem most recently solved always offers up a new one, then it will certainly please all who understand a gesture, an allusion and a gentle hint.[279]

Two days after this letter, on 22 July 1831, Goethe could note in his diary: *The main business finished. Last touches. Everything copied and fastened together.*[280] *Faust* was completed. One month later, he sealed up the manuscript, stipulating that it was to be published only after his death. *Faust, Part II of the Tragedy in Five Acts* appeared in 1833 as the first volume of his *Posthumous Works*.

Faust after Goethe

Since the early 19th century, more than a hundred versions of Faust have appeared, most of them in one way or another relating to Goethe's creation. Counted among the most significant are:

Lord Byron, *Manfred: A Dramatic Poem* (London, 1817)

Christian Dietrich Grabbe, *Don Juan und Faust. Eine Tragödie* [Don Juan and Faust: A Tragedy] (Frankfurt, 1829)

Nikolaus Lenau, *Faust. Ein Gedicht* [Faust: A Poem] (Stuttgart, 1836)

Heinrich Heine, *Der Doktor Faust. Ein Tanzpoem* [Doctor Faust: A Dance Poem] (Hamburg, 1851)

Imre Madách, *Az ember tragédiája* [The Tragedy of Man] (Budapest, 1861)

Friedrich Theodor Vischer, *Faust, der Tragödie dritter Teil* [Faust, Part Three of the Tragedy] (Tübingen, 1862)

Ferdinand Avenarius, *Faust. Ein Spiel* [Faust: A Play] (Munich, 1919)

Michel de Ghelderode, *La Mort du Docteur Faust* [The Death of Doctor Faust] (Bruges, 1926)

Paul Valéry, *Mon Faust* [My Faust] (Paris, 1945)

Thomas Mann, *Doktor Faustus* (Stockholm, 1947)

Hanns Eisler, *Johann Faustus. Oper* [Johann Faustus: An Opera] (Berlin, 1952)

Michel Butor, *Votre Faust. Fantaisie variable* [Your Faust: A Variable Fantasy] (Paris, 1962)

Lawrence Durrell, *An Irish Faustus: A Morality in Nine Scenes* (London, 1963)

Mikhail Bulgakov, *Master i Margarita* [The Master and Margarita] (Moscow, 1967)

Albert Paris Gütersloh, *Die Fabel von der Freundschaft* [The Fable of a Friendship] (Munich, 1969)]

Since then, the play has been interpreted by countless scholars, yet at times it seems as if its wealth of ideas, visions and allusions, the richness of expression and perception, still have not been fathomed. While some scenes are reminiscent of the chapbook tradition or, as in Faust's opening monologue, of Marlowe and his successors, Goethe's is different from all earlier versions: here the pact with the devil depends on a *Prologue in Heaven*. The two poles of the tragedy are the Lord, whose trust in human beings does not falter although at times they may stray, and Mephistopheles, now no longer just a devil hungry for souls, but a complex embodiment of scepticism. Within this framework, the actual pact between Faust and Mephistopheles involves the very Goethean concept of Faust's search for knowledge and whether it can ever be brought to an end by means of either self-satisfaction or sustained enjoyment. Thus Faust ventures the wager:

> *When on an idler's bed I stretch myself in quiet,*
> *then let, at once, my record end!*
> *Canst thou with lying flattery rule me,*
> *until self-pleased myself I see,*
> *canst thou with rich enjoyment fool me:*
> *let that day be the last for me!*
> *The bet I offer!*[281]

Seen from the vantage point of this pact, all events of the drama appear to be attempts by Mephistopheles to win Faust over with life's pleasures. The most important interludes along his way through *the common life and then the high*[282] are, in *Part I*, his love for Gretchen and the events that result from it; and in *Part II*, his appearance at the court of a powerful emperor, his journey to the *Mothers*[283] and his encounter with figures of Greek myth in the *Classical Walpurgis Night*, leading to a relationship with Helen of Troy, symbol of the purest beauty. Finally, in the fifth act of *Part II*, after saving the emperor from his enemies in battle, Faust requests as a reward the marshes along the coast of the realm in order to reclaim them for cultivation. One of the last scenes of the drama portrays Faust's vision of a free people who in the days to come would populate the newly-won land:

> *Anticipating here such lofty bliss,*
> *I now enjoy the highest Moment, – this.*[284]

With these words the hundred-year-old dies. Mephistopheles did not succeed in diverting him from his striving and hence lost the wager, not in its form but in its essence. Heavenly powers, figures from the *Christian-ecumenical*[285] world of faith, bear away *the immortal part of Faust.*[286]

A crucial aspect of the play is that its events take place not just in the external world, but even more in Faust's mind. Despite the variety of scenes and the multiplicity of happenings, Goethe's *Faust* is a psychological drama with a succession of inner experiences, struggles and doubts. In this regard, in June 1831, two weeks before the work was completed, Eckermann noted Goethe's explicit comment: 'We spoke then about the ending of *Faust*, and Goethe referred me to the passage that reads:[287]

> *The noble Spirit now is free,*
> *and saved from Evil's scheming:*
> *'Whoe'er aspires unweariedly*
> *is not beyond redeeming. '*
> *And if a love from up on high*
> *to him its grace is lending,*
> *the Blessèd Hosts that fill the sky*
> *shall welcome him, befriending.*[288]

CHORUS MYSTICUS
All that is transient
but as symbol is sent;
the unattainable
here is event;
the indescribable,
here it is done;
th'Eternal, in Woman
leads upward and on.

Closing stanzas of *Faust*. Translation by Bayard Taylor in Johann Wolfgang von Goethe, *Faust: Part Two*, ed. Stuart Atkins (New York, 1967)

In these verses, he said, *is the key to Faust's salvation. In Faust himself, increasingly more meaningful and pure activities prevail until the end, and from above, eternal love comes to his aid. This certainly is in harmony with our religious concept that we do not become blessed merely through our own powers but through supervening divine grace.'*[289]

Goethe spoke about *Faust* for the last time on 17 March 1832. A question from Wilhelm von Humboldt about the stages of his work elicited a detailed response. It is the last of the more than 15,000 letters that Goethe wrote over the course of his life: *More than sixty years ago, the concept of Faust was already clear to my youthful self, although the sequence of scenes was less distinct. I let the intent accompany me always, and worked only on those particular passages that interested me at the moment. Consequently, in the second part gaps remained that required a similar intensity of interest before they could be joined to the rest. Here the great obstacle was to achieve by means of resolve and willpower what really should have come from spontaneous action. But it would not be right if after such a long and reflective life this were not possible, and I don't allow myself to worry that people will be able to differentiate the older from the newer, the later from the earlier. This scrutiny we can pass on to future readers, if they are so inclined. Without question it would give me immeasurable pleasure if during my lifetime I could dedicate and communicate these very earnest jests to my valued and gratefully appreciated friends everywhere, and I should like to receive their responses. But the present age is indeed so absurd and confused that I persuade myself the honest*

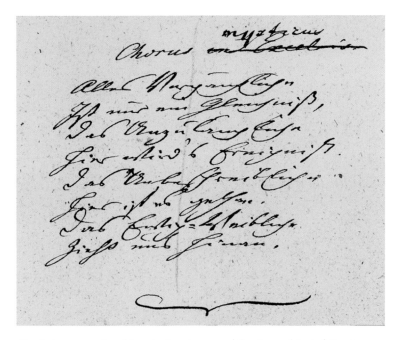

Goethe's manuscript of the closing stanzas of the *Second Part* of *Faust*. The original heading, which has been struck through, read *Chorus in Excelsis* [Chorus in the Highest]. Goethe altered it to *Chorus mysticus* [Mystical Chorus]. With a fine vertical line, Goethe's secretary indicated that he had transcribed the stanzas into the fair copy.

effort I have long expended on this curious edifice would be poorly rewarded. It would be beached, only to lie there like a wrecked ship, slowly becoming covered by the dunes of time. Muddled counsel about muddled action rules the world, and my most urgent task is to continue to develop whatever is and remains in me and to refine my own capabilities as much as possible – as you, worthy friend, also contrive to do. Forgive this delayed response! Despite my seclusion, there is seldom an hour in which to ponder those mysteries of life.[290]

Less than a week after dictating this letter, on 22 March 1832, half an hour before noon, Goethe died at the age of 82. On the following day Eckermann viewed the dead man: 'Stretched out on

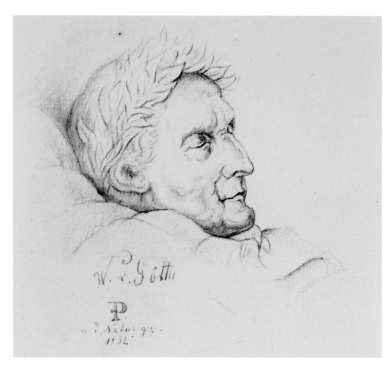

Friedrich Preller: Drawing of Goethe on the day of his funeral, 26 March 1832.

his back, he rested as if he were sleeping. Deep peace and strength lay over the features of his sublimely noble face. The powerful brow seemed still to harbour thought.'[291]

Notes

Numbers at the end of most notes
cite the volume and page of the
24-volume Artemis edition of
Goethe's works, selected letters and
conversations: *Gedenkausgabe der Werke,
Briefe und Gespräche* (Artemis, Zürich:
1948–1960). Two supplementary
volumes to the Artemis edition are
numbered 25 and 26. The abbreviation
WA in some of the notes refers to
the *Weimarer Ausgabe* [Weimar Edition]
of Goethe's works: *Goethes Werke*
(Hermann Böhlau, Weimar:
1887–1919). Other references
are listed with the relevant
bibliographical information.

1 Wieland, *An Psyche*. 22, 97.
2 *Dichtung und Wahrheit*, Part II,
    Book 7. 10, 312.
3 *Selbstcharakteristik*. 14, 185.
4 Letter to Wilhelm von
    Humboldt. 17 March 1832.
    21, 1043.
5 *Bildung und Umbildung organischer
    Naturen*. 1807. 17, 11.
6 *Dichtung und Wahrheit*, Part I,
    Book 1. 10, 21.
7 *Dichtung und Wahrheit*, Part I,
    Book 1. 10, 19.
8 *Dichtung und Wahrheit*, Part I,
    Book 1. 10, 18.
9 *Dichtung und Wahrheit*, Part I,
    Book 1. 10, 23.
10 *Dichtung und Wahrheit*, Part I,
    Book 1. 10, 22.
11 *Dichtung und Wahrheit*, Part I,
    Book 1. 10, 23.
12 *Dichtung und Wahrheit*, Part I,
    Book 1. 10, 23.
13 *Zahme Xenien*. 1, 669.
14 *Dichtung und Wahrheit*, Part II,
    Book 8. 10, 372.
15 *Zahme Xenien*. 1, 669.
16 *Zahme Xenien*. 1, 669.
17 *Dichtung und Wahrheit*, Part II,
    Book 6. 10, 254.
18 *Dichtung und Wahrheit*, Part II,
    Book 6. 10, 252.
19 *Dichtung und Wahrheit*, Part I,
    Book 1. 10, 43.
20 *Dichtung und Wahrheit*, Part I,
    Book 1. 10, 36.
21 *Dichtung und Wahrheit*, Part I,
    Book 2. 10, 54.
22 *Dichtung und Wahrheit*, Part I,
    Book 2. 10, 56.
23 *Dichtung und Wahrheit*, Part I,
    Book 2. 10, 55.
24 *An Personen*. 2, 194.
25 *Dichtung und Wahrheit*, Part II,
    Book 6. 10, 243.
26 *Dichtung und Wahrheit*, Part I,
    Book 5. 10, 222.
27 *Dichtung und Wahrheit*, Part II,
    Book 6. 10, 267.
28 *Dichtung und Wahrheit*, Part II,
    Book 6. 10, 270.
29 Letter to Riese. 20 October 1765.
    18, 17.
30 Letter to Riese. 23 April 1766.
    18, 32.
31 *Dichtung und Wahrheit*, Part II,
    Book 7. 10, 327.
32 *Dichtung und Wahrheit*, Part II,
    Book 7. 10, 328.
33 *Dichtung und Wahrheit*, Part II,
    Book 8. 10, 341.
34 *Dichtung und Wahrheit*, Part II,
    Book 7. 10, 296.

35 *Dichtung und Wahrheit*, Part II, Book 7. 10, 313.

36 *Dichtung und Wahrheit*, Part II, Book 7. 10, 312.

37 *Dichtung und Wahrheit*, Part II, Book 8. 10, 363.

38 *Dichtung und Wahrheit*, Part II, Book 8. 10, 370.

39 *Dichtung und Wahrheit*, Part II, Book 8. 10, 373.

40 Letter to Friederike Oeser. 13 February 1769. 18, 121.

41 *Von deutscher Baukunst.* 1772. 13, 21.

42 *Dichtung und Wahrheit*, Part III, Book 11. 10, 545.

43 *Dichtung und Wahrheit*, Part III, Book 11. 10, 517.

44 Letter to Hetzler. 24 August 1770. 18, 146.

45 Remark to Chancellor von Müller. 24 April 1830. 23, 690.

46 *Dichtung und Wahrheit*, Part II, Book 9. 10, 411.

47 *Dichtung und Wahrheit*, Part II, Book 10. 10, 444.

48 *Dichtung und Wahrheit*, Part III, Book 12. 10, 561.

49 *Dichtung und Wahrheit*, Part II, Book 10. 10, 448.

50 *Dichtung und Wahrheit*, Part II, Book 10. 10, 448.

51 *Dichtung und Wahrheit*, Part II, Book 10. 10, 474.

52 Letter to Friederike Brion. 15 October 1770. 18, 151.

53 *Dichtung und Wahrheit*, Part III, Book 11. 10, 496.

54 Letter to Herder. September 1771. 18, 162.

55 Letter to Salzmann. 19 June 1771. 18, 157.

56 *Dichtung und Wahrheit*, Part III, Book 11. 10, 518.

57 *Dichtung und Wahrheit*, Part III, Book 11. 10, 520.

58 *Dichtung und Wahrheit*, Part III, Book 12. 10, 569.

59 *Dichtung und Wahrheit*, Part III, Book 11. 10, 539.

60 *Dichtung und Wahrheit*, Part III, Book 11. 10, 536.

61 *Zum Schäkespears Tag.* 4, 126.

62 *Zum Schäkespears Tag.* 4, 124.

63 Letter to Herder. Early 1772. 18, 170.

64 Letter to Salzmann. 28 November 1771. 18, 168.

65 Letter to Salzmann. 28 November 1771. 18, 169.

66 Max Morris (ed.), *Der junge Goethe*, vol. 6. (Leipzig: 1912) p. 213.

67 *Dichtung und Wahrheit*, Part III, Book 12. 10, 570.

68 *Dichtung und Wahrheit*, Part III, Book 12. 10, 554.

69 Letter to Herder. 10 July 1772. 18, 173.

70 Johann Christian Kestner. May/June 1772. 22, 32.

71 *Dichtung und Wahrheit*, Part III, Book 12. 10, 607.

72 *Dichtung und Wahrheit*, Part III, Book 13. 10, 641.

73 Letter to Schönborn. 1 June 1774. 18, 227.

74 *Dichtung und Wahrheit*, Part III, Book 13. 10, 637.

75 *Die Leiden des jungen Werthers.* 4, 427.

76 *Zum Schäkespears Tag.* 4, 124.

77 Jacobi to Wieland. July 1774. 22, 65.

78 Letter to Auguste zu Stolberg. 7 March 1775. 18, 260.

79 *Dichtung und Wahrheit*, Part III, Book 15. 10, 698.

80 *Brief des Pastors.* 4, 134.

81 Letter to Anna Elisabeth von Türckheim. 14 December 1807. 19, 532.

82 Letter to Herder. 12 May 1775. WA IV. 2, 261.

83 Letter to Auguste von Bernstorff, née zu Stolberg. 17 April 1823. 21, 533.

84 Letter to Auguste zu Stolberg. 13 February 1775. 18, 257.

85 Letter to Herder. 25 March 1775. 18, 264.

86 *Dichtung und Wahrheit*, Part IV, Book 18. 10, 786.

87 *Dichtung und Wahrheit*, Part IV, Book 19. 10, 830.

88 *Stella*. Act III. 4, 903.

89 *Dichtung und Wahrheit*, Part IV, Book 20. 10, 847.

90 *Dichtung und Wahrheit*, Part IV, Book 20. 10, 841.

91 *Dichtung und Wahrheit*, Part IV, Book 20. 10, 842.

92 *Dichtung und Wahrheit*, Part IV, Book 20. 10, 852.

93 *Tagebücher*. 30 October 1775. 26, 13.

94 Remark to Eckermann. 10 February 1829. 24, 311.

95 *Zum feierlichen Andenken Anna Amalias*. 12, 690.

96 Remark to Eckermann. 23 October 1828. 24, 697.

97 Remark to Chancellor von Müller. August 1830. 23, 720.

98 Letter to Johanna Fahlmer. 14 February 1776. 18, 308.

99 Wilhelm Bode, *Goethes Leben im Garten am Stern* (Mittler, Berlin:1901) p. 38.

100 Letter to Catharina Elisabeth Goethe. 11 August 1781. 18, 611.

101 Letter to Merck. 22 January 1777. 18, 304.

102 *Dichtung und Wahrheit*. 10, 874.

103 *Tagebücher*. 13 January 1779. 26, 72.

104 *Wilhelm Meisters Wanderjahre*, Book III, Chapter 13. 8, 457.

105 Letter to Knebel. 3. December 1781. 18, 626.

106 Letter to Johanna Fahlmer. 14 February 1776. 18, 308.

107 Letter to Wieland. April 1776. 18, 320.

108 Untitled, translated by Edwin H. Zeydel in *Goethe, the Lyrist*, ed. Edwin H. Zeydel, 2nd ed. (University of North Carolina Press, Chapel Hill: 1955) p. 58-61, hereafter *Goethe, the Lyrist*.

109 *Tagebücher*. 14 November 1777. 26, 52.

110 *Tagebücher*. 13 March 1778. 26, 60.

111 *Tagebücher*. Early April 1778. 26, 61.

112 *Tagebücher*. 15 March 1778. 26, 60.

113 *Tagebücher*. 16 January 1778. 26, 58.

114 *Tagebücher*. Early February 1778. 26, 59.

115 *Iphigenie*. Act IV, Scene 4. 6, 136.

116 *Tagebücher*. 14 November 1777. 26, 52.

117 *Iphigenie*. Act IV, Scene 4. 6, 136.

118 *Tagebücher*. Late December 1778. 26, 69.

119 *Iphigenie*. Act V, Scene 3. 6, 140.

120 *Tagebücher*. Late December 1778. 26, 70.

121 *Iphigenie*. Act V, Scene 3. 6, 142.

122 *Tagebücher*. 7 August 1779. 26, 85.

123 *Tagebücher*. 25 July 1779. 26, 82.

124 *Tagebücher*. 18 January 1780. 26, 93.

125 *Tagebücher*. 19 Jan. 1780. 26, 93.

126 *Tagebücher*. 13 May 1770. 26, 102.

127 *Tagebücher*. November 1781. 26, 114.

128 Letter to Lavater. 20 September 1780. 18, 532.

129 *Tagebücher*. 26 March 1780. 26, 98.

130 *Tagebücher*. Late April 1780. 26, 101.

131 *Tagebücher*. 13 January 1779. 26, 72.

132 Letter to Charlotte von Stein. 4 June 1782. 18, 671.

133 *Tagebücher*. 30 March 1787. 26, 99.

134 Remark to Caroline Herder. March 1789. 22, 182.

135 *Tagebücher*. 20 November 1780. 26, 109.

136 Letter to Krafft. 31 Jan. 1781. 18, 564.

137 Letter to Herzog Carl August. 2 September 1786. 19, 14.

138 *Tagebücher*. 3 September 1786. 26, 123.

139 *Tagebücher*. 3 September 1786. 26, 123.

140 Letter to Duchess Louise. Rome, 23 December 1786. 19, 44.

141 *Tagebücher*. Venice, 10 October 1786. 26, 175.

142 *Tag- und Jahreshefte*. 1789. 11, 623.

143 *Tagebücher*. Trento, 11 September 1786. 26, 138.

144 *Italienische Reise*. Venice, 28 September 1786. 11, 69.

145 *Tagebücher*. Bologna, 18 October 1786. 26, 180.

146 *Italienische Reise*. Rome, 1 November 1786. 11, 137.

147 *Italienische Reise*. Rome, 5 November 1786. 11, 142.

148 Letter to Charlotte von Stein. 23 December 1786. WA IV. 8, 100.

149 Letter to Charlotte von Stein. 6 January 1787. 19, 51.

150 *Italienische Reise*. Rome, 2 December 1786. 11, 159.

151 Letter to Charlotte von Stein. 23 December 1786. WA IV. 8, 101.

152 *Italienische Reise*. Rome, 6 September 1787. 11, 436.

153 Letter to Herder. Rome, 10 November 1786. 19, 29.

154 Wilhelm Tischbein. Rome, December 1786. 22, 158.

155 *Italienische Reise*. Naples, 23 March 1787. 11, 240.

156 *Italienische Reise*. Naples, 23 March 1787. 11, 240.

157 *Italienische Reise*. Naples, 20 March 1787. 11, 236.

158 *Italienische Reise*. Palermo, 13 April 1787. 11, 275.

159 *Italienische Reise*. Naples, 17 May 1787. 11, 353.

160 *Italienische Reise*. Sicily, May 1787. 11, 328.

161 Charlotte von Stein to Knebel. Late April 1784. 22, 143.

162 *Geschichte meines botanischen Studiums*. 17, 80.

163 *Italienische Reise*. Naples, 17 May 1787. 11, 353.

164 *Italienische Reise*. Zweiter Römischer Aufenthalt. 11, 383.

165 *Italienische Reise*. Rome, November 1787. 11, 480.

166 *Italienische Reise*. Rome, October 1787. 11, 465.

167 *Italienische Reise*. Rome, 25 December 1787. 11, 492.

168 *Italienische Reise*. Rome, November 1787. 11, 484.

169 *Italienische Reise*. Rome, April 1788. 11, 611.

170 *Geschichte meines botanischen Studiums*. 17, 84.

171 Letter to Charlotte von Stein. 23 December 1786. WA IV. 8, 102.

172 Letter from Caroline Herder to her husband. 4 September 1788. 22, 70.

173 Letter from Schiller to Körner. 12. September 1788, in Wolfgang Herwig (ed.), *Goethes Gespräche* (Artemis, Zürich: 1965) vol. 1, p. 444.

174 Letter from Schiller to Körner. 1788/89. 22, 178.

175 Letter from Charlotte von Stein to Friedrich von Stein. 17 May 1796, in Renate Grumach (ed.) *Goethe, Begegnungen und Gespräche* (De Gruyter, Berlin: 1980) vol. 4, p. 222.

176 Letter to Knebel. Weimar, 9 July 1790. 19, 168.

177 *Die Metamorphose der Pflanzen*. 17, 56.

178 *Zur Morphologie. Paralipomena*. WA II. 6, 446.

179 *Tag- und Jahreshefte*. 1789. 11, 622.

180 Remark to Eckermann. 4 January 1824. 24, 549.

181 *Kampagne in Frankreich*. 3 September 1792. 12, 266.

182 *Kampagne in Frankreich*. 19 September 1792. 12, 289.

183 *Belagerung von Mainz*. 25 July 1793. 12, 455.

184 Letter to John. 27 November 1813. WA IV. 24, 48.

185 *Glückliches Ereignis*. 16, 864.

186 *Erste Bekanntschaft mit Schiller*. 12, 620.

187 *Erste Bekanntschaft mit Schiller*. 12, 622.

188 *Erste Bekanntschaft mit Schiller*.
12, 622.

189 *Erste Bekanntschaft mit Schiller*.
12, 622.

190 Letter from Schiller to Goethe.
23 August 1794. 20, 13.

191 Letter to Schiller. 27 August
1794. 20, 16.

192 *Erste Bekanntschaft mit Schiller*.
12, 619.

193 Letter to Schiller. 27 August
1794. 20, 17.

194 Remark to Eckermann. 24 March
1829. 24, 331.

195 Letter from Schiller to Körner.
1 February 1796, in Friedrich
Schiller, *Schillers Werke:
Nationalausgabe* (Hermann
Böhlau, Weimar: 1948-) vol. 28,
p. 178.

196 *Erste Bekanntschaft mit Schiller*.
12, 623.

197 Philipp Otto Runge, *Hinterlassene
Schriften* (Perthes, Hamburg:
1840) Part 1, p. 6.

198 *Tag- und Jahreshefte*. 1805. 11, 747.

199 *Tag- und Jahreshefte*. 1805. 11, 749.

200 Letter to Zelter. 1. June 1805.
19, 479.

201 *Epilog zu Schillers Glocke*. 2, 96.

202 *Gedichte*. 1, 522.

203 Letter to Knebel. 24 December
1824. 21, 620.

204 Remark to Eckermann. 14 March
1830. 24, 731.

205 *Tagebücher*. 14 October 1806.
26, 270.

206 Letter to Günther. 17 October
1806. 19, 498.

207 *Unterredung mit Napoleon*. 12, 636.

208 *Entwurf einer Farbenlehre*. 16, 20.

209 *Polarität*. 16, 863.

210 Remark to Riemer. 24 March
1807. 22, 444.

211 *Tag- und Jahreshefte*. 1811.
11, 846.

212 Remark to Riemer. 28 August
1808, 22, 500.

213 Letter from Kleist to Goethe, 24
Jan. 1808, in Karl Robert
Mandelkow (ed.), *Briefe an Goethe*

(Beck, München: 1982) vol. 1,
496, hereafter *Briefe an Goethe*.

214 Letter to Zelter. 20 October
1831. 21, 1013.

215 Letter from Sulpiz Boisserée to
his brother. 4 May 1811. 22, 628.

216 Remark to Riemer. 24 July 1809.
22, 565.

217 Letter to Beethoven. 25 June
1811. 19, 637.

218 *Tagebücher*. 21 July 1812.
26, 318.

219 Letter to Zelter. 2 September
1812. 19, 672.

220 *Tag- und Jahreshefte*. 1815.
11, 867.

221 Remark to Bertram. 26.
September 1814. 22, 764.

222 *Tag- und Jahreshefte*. 1815.
11, 868.

223 *West-östlicher Divan*. 3, 361.

224 *West-östlicher Divan*. 3, 344.

225 *Seelige Sehnsucht*, translated by
Michael Hamburger in Johann
Wolfgang von Goethe, *Selected
Poems*, ed. Christopher Middleton
(John Calder, London: 1983) p.
207, hereafter *Selected Poems*, ed.
Middleton.

226 Remark to Bertram. 26.
September 1814. 22, 764.

227 *Kunst und Altertum am Rhein und
Main*. 12, 594.

228 *Kunst und Altertum am Rhein und
Main*. 12, 523.

229 Letter to Charlotte von Stein. 23
December 1786. WA IV. 8, 101.

230 *Tagebücher*. 6 June 1816. 26, 344.

231 *Tagebücher*. 31 December 1822.
26, 411.

232 Letter to Zelter. 3 May 1816.
21, 157.

233 Letter to Boisserée. 3 February
1826. 21, 677.

234 *Dichtung und Wahrheit*, Part II,
Book 8. 10, 381.

235 *West-östlicher Divan*. 3, 295.

236 Remark to Eckermann. 27
January 1824. 24, 83.

237 Remark to Lang. Mid-year 1826.
23, 540.

238 *Tagebücher*. 30 January 1823. 26, 412.

239 Remark to Eckermann. 27 October 1823. 24, 60.

240 *Marienbader Elegie*. 1, 477.

241 *Marienbader Elegie*. 1, 475.

242 *Elegy*, translated by John Whaley in Johann Wolfgang von Goethe, *Selected Poems* (Dent, London: 1998) p. 138–141.

243 Letter to Zelter. 4 September 1831. 21, 998.

244 Letter to Humboldt. 1 December 1831. 21, 1024.

245 Remark to Eckermann. 17 February 1832. 24, 767.

246 Remark to Eckermann. 17 February 1832. 24, 768.

247 Remark to Eckermann. 2 January 1824. 24, 544.

248 Remark to Eckermann. 2 January 1824. 24, 545.

249 *Wilhelm Meisters Wanderjahre*, Book III, 13. 8, 460.

250 Letter to Zelter. 6 June 1825. 21, 633.

251 Letter to Zelter. 6 June 1825. 21, 634.

252 Remark to Eckermann. 21 February 1827. 24, 599.

253 Letter to Knebel. 9 November 1814. 21, 35.

254 Remark to Eckermann. 31 January 1827. 24, 228.

255 *Allgemeine Betrachtungen zur Weltliteratur*. 14, 914.

256 *Dichtung und Wahrheit* Part III, Book 15. 10, 695.

257 Letter to Jacobi. 6 January 1813. 19, 689.

258 Letter to Jacobi. 6 January 1813. 19, 689.

259 Letter from Auguste von Bernstorff née zu Stolberg to Goethe. 15 October 1822, in *Briefe an Goethe*, vol. 2, p. 338.

260 Letter to Auguste von Bernstorff née zu Stolberg. 17 April 1823. 21, 533.

261 Remark to Eckermann. 11 March 1832. 24, 771.

262 Remark to Eckermann. 11 March 1832. 24, 772.

263 *Testament*, translated by Christopher Middleton in *Selected Poems*, ed. Middleton, p. 266-269.

264 Letter to Boisserée. 22 March 1831. 21, 976.

265 Letter to Zelter. 14 December 1830. 21, 953.

266 Letter to Zelter. 19 March 1827. 21, 728.

267 Letter to Zelter. 21 November 1830. 21, 949.

268 Letter to Zelter. 14 December 1830. 21, 952.

269 Letter to Sigismund von Herder. 19 Jan. 1831. WA IV. 48, 90.

270 Letter to Zelter. 14 December 1830. 21, 952.

271 Letter to Zelter. 14 December 1830. 21, 952.

272 Letter to Zelter. 21 November 1830. 21, 950.

273 Letter to Reinhard. 7 September 1831. 21, 1001.

274 Report by Mahr. 27 August 1831. 23, 769. Verse translation by Henry Wadsworth Longfellow in *Selected Poems*, ed. Middleton, p. 59.

275 Letter from Schiller to Goethe. 29 November 1794. 20, 42.

276 Letter to Schiller. 2 December 1794. 20, 43.

277 Letter to Schiller. 22 June 1797. 20, 361.

278 *Tagebücher*. 10 November 1828. 25, 498.

279 Letter to Meyer. 20 July 1831. 5, 664.

280 *Tagebücher*. 22 July 1831. 26, 566.

281 *Faust*, line 1692. Johann Wolfgang von Goethe, *Faust: Part One*. The Bayard Taylor translation, revised and edited by Stuart Atkins (Collier, New York: 1962) p. 94, hereafter *Faust I*.

282 *Faust*, line 2052. *Faust I*, p. 103.

283 *Faust*, line 6216. Johann Wolfgang von Goethe, *Faust: Part Two*. The

Bayard Taylor translation, revised and edited by Stuart Atkins (Collier, New York: 1967) p. 59, hereafter *Faust II*.

284 *Faust*, line 11585. *Faust II*, p. 223.

285 Remark to Eckermann. 6 June 1831. 24, 504.

286 *Faust*, line 11824. *Faust II*, p. 229.

287 Remark to Eckermann. 6 June 1831. 24, 504.

288 *Faust*, line 11934. *Faust II*, p. 233.

289 Remark to Eckermann. 6 June 1831. 24, 504.

290 Letter to Humboldt. 17 March 1832. 21, 1042.

291 Eckermann. 23 March 1832. 24, 511.

Chronology

Year	Date	Life

Titles of Goethe's works are *italicized*. Dates for the works refer to the year of creation, unless otherwise noted.

1749	28 August	Johann Wolfgang Goethe born at Frankfurt am Main.

1755	1 November	Lisbon earthquake.

1759	January to February 1763	Occupation of Frankfurt by French troops.

1764	3 April	Goethe observes celebrations surrounding the coronation of Joseph II.

1765	October to August 1768	Studies at Leipzig. Friendships with Käthchen Schönkopf, Stock, Oeser. *The Lover's Caprices* (Die Laune des Verliebten).

1767		Friendship with Behrisch.

1768	July / 28 August / September to March 1770	Severe illness. Departure from Leipzig. Convalescence in Frankfurt. *The Accomplices* (Die Mitschuldigen).

Year	History	Culture
1749	First settlement of Ohio Company. Establishment of Halifax, Nova Scotia, as fortress.	Handel, *Music for the Royal Fireworks*. Gainsborough, *Mr. and Mrs. Robert Andrews*.
1755	1756–1763 Seven Years War.	Samuel Johnson, *Dictionary of the English Language* (–1773).
1759	Jesuits expelled from Portugal.	Samuel Johnson, *Rasselas*. Voltaire, *Candide*.
1764	Coronation in Frankfurt of Joseph II as Holy Roman Emperor.	Mozart (aged eight) writes his first symphony.
1765	British Parliament passes Stamp Act for taxing American colonies; Virginia Assembly challenges the tax.	Boucher becomes court painter at Versailles. Horace Walpole, *The Castle of Otranto*.
1767	British introduce taxes on imports into the American colonies.	Gluck, *Alceste*.
1768	France buys Corsica from Genoa.	Founding of Royal Academy, London, with J. Reynolds as president. A. Canaletto dies. Mozart's first opera given in Vienna.

Year	Date	Life
1770	April to August 1771	Studies in Strasbourg.
	October	First visit to Sesenheim. Friendship with Friederike Brion.
1771	6 August	Awarded Licentiate of Law degree.
	Mid-August	Return to Frankfurt. *On Shakespeare's Day* (Zum Schäkespears Tag).
1772	May-September	Intern at the Imperial Supreme Court in Wetzlar. Friendship with Charlotte Buff.
1773		*Letter of the Pastor* (Brief des Pastors). *Götz von Berlichingen*.
1774	July-August	Journey along the Lahn and Rhine rivers. *The Sorrows of Young Werther* (Die Leiden des jungen Werthers).
1775	April	Engagement to Lili Schönemann.
	May-July	Journey to Switzerland.
	Early autumn	Termination of the engagement.
	30 October	Departure from Frankfurt.
	7 November	Arrival in Weimar.
	November	First encounter with Charlotte von Stein.

Year	History	Culture
1770	Dauphin of France marries Marie Antoinette, daughter of Maria Theresa of Austria.	Edmund Burke, *Thoughts on the Causes of the Present Discontents*.
1771	Russia and Prussia agree about partition of Poland. Russia completes conquest of the Crimea.	Haydn, *Sun* quartets. Klopstock, *Odes*.
1772	Samuel Adams forms Committees of Correspondence in Massachusetts for action against Great Britain.	Lessing, E*milia Galotti*. Herder, *On the Origin of Speech*. Mozart, *Lucio Silla*.
1773	Boston Tea Party: American colonists protest against British tax.	Herder, *Of German Ways and Art* (manifesto of Storm and Stress).
1774	Accession of Louis XVI of France.	Gluck, *Iphigénie en Aulide*.
1775	American Revolution begins (−1783). England hires 29,000 German mercenaries for war in North America.	G. Romney becomes fashionable painter in London. J. Watt perfects his invention of the steam engine.

Year	Date	Life
1776	January-February	Decision to remain in Weimar for an unspecified period of time.
	April	Residency in the garden house on the banks of the Ilm, until June 1782.
	11 June	Formal entry into the Weimar civil service.
1777	December:	Trip on horseback through the Harz Mountains. *Harz Journey in Winter* (Harzreise im Winter).
1778	May	Journey with Duke Carl August to Berlin and Potsdam.
1779	September to January 1780	Journey to Switzerland with Duke Carl August. *Iphigenia in Tauris* (Iphigenie auf Tauris) in prose.
1780		Growing interest in mineralogical studies.
1781	August	Work on *Torquato Tasso*.
	November	Weekly lectures on anatomy in the Weimar Academy of Arts.

Year	History	Culture
1776	Declaration of Independence of the United States of America.	Adam Smith, *An Inquiry into the Nature and Causes of the Wealth of Nations*.
1777	Congress adopts Confederation Articles, which are sent to states for ratification as first US constitution.	Haydn, *La Roxolane* Symphony. Gluck, *Armide*.
1778	War of Bavarian Succession.	Voltaire, *Irène*.
1779	Spain declares war on Britain and the siege of Gibraltar opens.	S. Johnson, *Lives of the Poets*. Lessing, *Nathan the Wise*.
1780	Serfdom in Bohemia and Hungary abolished. Maria Theresa of Austria dies, succeeded by Joseph II.	Haydn, *Toy* Symphony. Frederick II, *De la Littérature allemande*. *The British Gazette and Sunday Monitor*: first Sunday newspaper.
1781	Joseph II declares himself 'Enlightened Despot' in effort to modernise Holy Roman Empire. Charles Cornwallis surrenders at Yorktown; end of American Revolution.	William Herschel discovers Uranus. Mozart, *Idomeneo*. Schiller, *The Robbers*. Kant, *Critique of Pure Reason*. Pestalozzi, *Leonard and Gertrude*.

Year	Date	Life
1782	2 June	Move to the house at the Frauenplan.
	3 June	Receipt of a patent of nobility bestowed by Emperor Joseph II.
1783	September-October	Journey to the Harz Mountains, to Göttingen and Kassel.
1784	March	Discovery of the intermaxillary bone in humans.
1785	June-August	At Carlsbad. *Wilhelm Meister's Theatrical Calling* (Wilhelm Meisters theatralische Sendung).
1786	July-August	At Carlsbad.
	3 September	Departure from Carlsbad for Italy.
	29 October	Arrival in Rome. *Iphigenia in Tauris*, in verse.
1787	February-June	Journey to Naples and Sicily.
1788	23 April	Departure from Rome.
	18 June	Return to Weimar.
	July	Liaison with Christiane Vulpius. *Roman Elegies* (Römische Elegien).

Year	History	Culture
1782	James Watt patents double-acting rotary steam engine.	Mozart, *Haffner* Symphony and *Il Seraglio*.
1783	Treaty of Versailles between Britain, France, Spain and US.	Montgolfier brothers take first hot-air balloon flight.
1784	Treaty of Constantinople: Russia annexes Crimea.	Henry Cavendish discovers that water is a compound rather than an element. Herder, *Ideas towards a Philosophy of History*.
1785	Steam engine with rotary motion installed by M. Boulton and J. Watt in a cotton-spinning factory in Nottinghamshire.	Mozart, six string quartets dedicated to Haydn.
1786	Frederick II dies, succeeded by Frederick William II.	Mozart, *The Marriage of Figaro*. Robert Burns, *Poems chiefly in the Scottish Dialect*.
1787	Catherine II visits the Crimea, sees in passing Potemkin's artificial villages.	Mozart, *Don Giovanni*. Schiller, *Don Carlos*.
1788	First British penal settlement is founded at Botany Bay. US constitution comes into force.	John Walter founds *The Times*. Kant, *Critique of Practical Reason* ('Categorical Imperative').

Year	Date	Life
1789	25 December	Birth of Goethe's son August. *Torquato Tasso.*
1790		*The Metamorphosis of Plants* (Die Metamorphose der Pflanzen).
1791	January	Appointed Director of the Weimar Court Theatre. *Reflections on Optics* (Beiträge zur Optik).
1792	August-October 19 September	Participation in the Allies' campaign against France. Bombardment of Valmy.
1793	May-July	Observer at the siege of Mainz. *The Citizen-General* (Der Bürgergeneral). *Reynard the Fox* (Reineke Fuchs).

Year	History	Culture
1789	French Revolution. George Washington inaugurated as US president (until 1797). Antoine Lavoisier establishes modern chemistry.	Mozart, *Così fan tutte*. William Blake, *Songs of Innocence*.
1790	Death of Emperor Joseph II; Leopold II becomes Holy Roman Emperor.	Kant, *Critique of Judgement*. Robert Burns, *Tam O'Shanter*.
1791	Counter-revolutionaries organise military invasion of France from Germany. US Congress meets in Philadelphia; selects site of District of Columbia. P. D. Toussaint-Louverture leads slave revolt in Haiti.	Mozart, *Magic Flute* and *Requiem*. Haydn, *Surprise* Symphony. Thomas Paine, *The Rights of Man*.
1792	French National Assembly's declaration of war against Austria; Revolutionary Commune established in Paris; mob invades Tuileries; royal family imprisoned; French Republic proclaimed; the Jacobins, under G. J. Danton, wrest power from the Girondins.	Mary Wollstonecraft, *Vindication of the Rights of Women*. C. J. Rouget de Lisle, 'La Marseillaise'.
1793	Seige of French-occupied Mainz by the allies. Withdrawal of the French army. Louis XVI executed. Reign of Terror under Robespierre in France. Second partition of Poland. Marie Antoinette executed.	Kant, *Religion within the Boundaries of Reason*. The Louvre, Paris, becomes a national art gallery.

Year	Date	Life
1794	Late July	Discussion with Schiller about the primal plant.
1795	July-August	At Carlsbad.
1796		*Wilhelm Meister's Apprenticeship* (Wilhelm Meisters Lehrjahre). *Hermann and Dorothea* (Hermann und Dorothea).
1797	August-November	Third journey to Switzerland. *Ballads* (Balladen). Resumption of work on *Faust*.
1798	12 October	Opening of the remodelled Court Theatre with *Wallenstein's Encampment* (Wallensteins Lager) by Schiller.

Year	History	Culture
1794	Robespierre executed. Eli Whitney patents cotton-gin in US. Abolition of slavery in French colonies.	Blake, *Songs of Experience*. Xavier De Maistre, *Voyage autour de ma chambre*.
1795	Peace concluded between France and Prussia. Methodists formally split from the Church of England. Third partition of Poland. Directory government in France. Whiskey Rebellion in US. Hydraulic press invented in Britain.	John Soane begins the Bank of England building. First performance of Haydn *London* Symphony.
1796	Edward Jenner discovers smallpox vaccine.	Goya, *Los Caprichos*. Fanny Burney, *Camilla*.
1797	John Adams inaugurated as US president. Treaty of Campo Formio. France creates Cisalpine Republic and annexes left bank of Rhine.	M. L. C. Cherubini, *Medea*. S. T. Coleridge, *Kubla Khan*. A. W. von Schlegel begins his Shakespeare translation into German. Turner, *Millbank, Moon Light*.
1798	1798-1801 Second war against France waged by a coalition of Austria, England and Russia. France invades Egypt.	Alois Senefelder invents lithography. Wordsworth and Coleridge, *Lyrical Ballads*.

Year	Date	Life
1799	February-April	In Jena work on the *Theory of Colours* (Farbenlehre).
	December	Schiller moves from Jena to Weimar.
1800	April-May	Journey with Duke Carl August to Leipzig.
1801	January	Attack of facial erysipelas.
	June-August	Journey to Pyrmont, Göttingen and Kassel.
1802	January-June	Frequently at Jena.
1803		*The Natural Daughter* (Die natürliche Tochter).
1804		*Winckelmann and His Age* (Winckelmann und sein Jahrhundert).

Year	History	Culture
1799	Napoleon defeats the Turks at Aboukir and assumes control of France as First Consul.	Beethoven, *Pathétique* Sonata.
1800	Napoleon defeats Austrians at the Battle of Marengo and reconquers Italy.	Alessandro Volta makes first battery. William Wordsworth's manifesto of romanticism. Novalis, *To the Night*.
1801	Thomas Jefferson inaugurated as US president. Irish Act of Union. Napoleon and Pope Pius VII sign concordat. Alexander I becomes tsar of Russia.	Haydn, *The Seasons*. Chateaubriand, *Atala*.
1802	Napoleon annexes Piedmont, Parma and Piacenza.	Mme. de Staël, *Delphine*.
1803	Louisiana Purchase. First steam rail locomotive line built, in south Wales.	Beethoven, *Kreutzer* Sonata. Tieck, *Minnelieder*.
1804	Pope crowns Napoleon emperor. Haiti becomes independent. Civil Code created in France.	Blake, *Jerusalem*. Beethoven, *Symphony No. 3*. Schiller, *Wilhelm Tell*.

Year	Date	Life
1805	January-February	Attacks of renal colic.
	9 May	Death of Schiller.
	July-September	Repeatedly at Bad Lauchstädt.
		Epilogue to Schiller's 'Bell'
		(Epilog zu Schillers 'Glocke').
1806	April	Completion of *Faust, Part One* (Faust, Erster Teil).
	14 October	Battle of Jena and Auerstedt. Occupation of Weimar by the French.
	19 October	Marriage to Christiane Vulpius.
1807	May-September	At Carlsbad.
		Sonnets (Sonette).
1808	May-September	At Carlsbad and Franzensbad.
	2 October	Audience with Napoleon at Erfurt.
1809		*Elective Affinities* (Die Wahlverwandtschaften).
1810	May-September	At Carlsbad, Teplitz, Dresden.
		Theory of Colours (Farbenlehre).
1811	May-June	At Carlsbad with Christiane.
		Poetry and Truth, Part One (Dichtung und Wahrheit, Erster Teil).

Year	History	Culture
1805	Battle of the Three Emperors, near Austerlitz: Napoleon defeats Austria and Russia. Battle of Trafalgar.	Wordsworth, *The Prelude*. Turner, *Shipwreck*.
1806	Francis II relinquishes the Imperial crown. Dissolution of the Holy Roman Empire of the German Nation.	Jean-Dominique Ingres, *Napoleon on the Imperial Throne*.
1807	Baron vom Stein becomes Prussian Prime Minister and emancipates serfs.	Hegel, *Phenomenology of Mind*. David, *Coronation of Napoleon*.
1808	French armies occupy Rome and invade Spain.	C. D. Friedrich, *The Cross on the Mountains*. Beethoven, *Symphonies No. 5* and *No. 6*.
1809	War between France and Austria.	Constable, *Malvern Hill*.
1810	Year of Napoleon's zenith.	Beethoven, Music to Goethe's *Egmont*.
1811	George III of England insane; Prince of Wales becomes Prince Regent.	J. Austen, *Sense and Sensibility*.

Year	Date	Life
1812	May-September	At Carlsbad and Teplitz. Meeting with Beethoven. *Poetry and Truth, Part Two* (Dichtung und Wahrheit, Zweiter Teil).
1813	April-August	At Teplitz. *Poetry and Truth, Part Three* (Dichtung und Wahrheit, Dritter Teil).
1814	July-October	Journey to the Rhine and Main regions. Encounter with Marianne von Willemer. Visits to the Boisserée brothers in Heidelberg.
1815	February	Congress of Vienna proclaims Sachsen-Weimar Eisenach a Grand Duchy.
	May-October	Second journey to the Rhine and Main area.
1816	6 June	Death of Christiane. *Italian Journey* (Italienische Reise).

Year	History	Culture
1812	Napoleon's campaign against Russia. Burning of Moscow, retreat of the French.	J. and W. Grimm, *Fairy Tales*. Hegel, *Logic*.
1813	Battle of the Nations, near Leipzig.	J. Austen, *Pride and Prejudice*. Lord Byron, *Childe Harold's Pilgrimage*. G. Rossini, *Tancredi*.
1814	1814-1815 Congress of Vienna.	Goya, *The Second of May* and *The Third of May 1808*. Ingres, *L'Odalisque*. Beethoven, *Fidelio*. Schubert begins Lied production.
1815	Battle of Waterloo: Wellington's and Blücher's victory over Napoleon. Napoleon exiled to St. Helena.	Nash rebuilds Brighton Pavilion. Turner, *Crossing the Brook*. The Biedermeier style arrives (–1848).
1816	Federation of major German states under Austrian guidance (Deutscher Bund), with irregular meetings in Frankfurt am Main.	J. Austen, *Emma*. S. T. Coleridge, 'Kubla Khan'. G. Rossini, *The Barber of Seville*.

Year	Date	Life
1817	March-August, November	Often in Jena.
	17 June	Marriage of August von Goethe to Ottilie von Pogwisch. *History of My Botanical Studies* (Geschichte meines botanischen Studiums).
1818	July-September	At Carlsbad.
1819	August-September	At Carlsbad. *West-Eastern Divan* (West-östlicher Divan).
1820	April-May	At Carlsbad.
1821	July-September	At Marienbad and Eger. Encounter with Ulrike von Levetzow.

Year	History	Culture
1817	Student societies protest at the Wartburg calling for more liberal rule by German states.	Hegel, *Encyclopaedia of the Philosophical Sciences*. D. Ricardo, *Principles of Political Economy*.
1818	Allies evacuate their troops from France. Chile proclaims its independence.	J. Austen, *Persuasion*. M. Shelley, *Frankenstein*. Prado museum opens in Madrid.
1819	Carlsbad Resolution Decrees aimed at suppressing students' protests.	Schubert, *Trout Quintet*. J. Keats, 'Ode to a Nightingale' . A. Schopenhauer, *World as Will and Idea*. T. Gericault, *Raft of the Medusa*.
1820	Revolution in Spain and Portugal – both demand constitutions.	W. Scott, *Ivanhoe*. P. B. Shelley, *Prometheus Unbound*. Venus de Milo is discovered.
1821	1821–1829 Greek struggle for independence from Turkish domination.	J. Constable, *The Hay Wain*. T. De Quincey, *Confessions of an English Opium-Eater*. Hegel, *Philosophy of Right*.

Year	Date	Life
1822	June-August	At Marienbad and Eger. *Campaign in France* (Kampagne in Frankreich).
1823	February-March 10 June July-September	Pericarditis. Eckermann's first visit to Goethe. At Marienbad, Eger and Carlsbad.
1824		Preparations for publication of the *Correspondence with Schiller* (Briefwechsel mit Schiller).
1825	February	Resumption of work on *Faust*.
1826		The 'Helen' act in *Faust*.
1827		During the year Goethe receives many visitors, including King Ludwig I of Bavaria.
1828	14 June	Death of Grand Duke Carl August.

Year	History	Culture
1822	Brazil becomes independent from Portugal.	A. Pushkin, *Eugene Onegin* (until 1832).
1823	The Monroe Doctrine closes the American continents to colonial settlements by European powers.	Beethoven finishes *Missa Solemnis*. Schubert, *Rosamunde*.
1824	First Burmese War: British take Rangoon. Egyptians capture Crete. Turks defeated at Mitylene.	Heine, *Harz Journey*. Leopardi, *Canzoni*.
1825	French law compensates the aristocrats for losses in the Revolution. Decembrist revolt in Russia crushed.	A. Manzoni, *I promessi sposi*. Pushkin, *Boris Godunov*.
1826	Commercial treaty between Prussia and Mecklenburg-Schwerin begins the idea of a customs union (Zollverein).	Eichendorff, *Memoirs of a Good-for-Nothing*. Weber, *Oberon*.
1827	Russia, France and Britain urge Turkey to end war with Greece; their note is rejected by the Sultan.	Scott, *Life of Napoleon Buonaparte*. Schubert, *Winterreise*. Hugo, *Hernani*.
1828	Establishment of customs unions among various German states.	Rossini, *Le Conte Ory*. Delacroix, Illustrations to *Faust*. A. Dumas (père), *Les Trois Mousquetaires*.

Year	Date	Life
1829		*Wilhelm Meister's Journeyman Years* (Wilhelm Meisters Wanderjahre).
1830	10 November	News of his son's death in Rome reaches Goethe; he suffers a haemorrhage in late November. *Poetry and Truth, Part Four* (Dichtung und Wahrheit, Vierter Teil).
1831	22 July	*Faust, Part Two* completed.
	28 August	Goethe's last birthday, spent in Ilmenau.
1832	22 March	Death of Goethe.

Year	History	Culture
1829	Slavery abolished in Mexico.	W. Irving, *The Conquest of Granada*.
1830	July Revolution in Paris. Unrest in central Germany.	The religious society of Mormons founded by Joseph Smith at Fayette, N.Y.
1831	Prince Leopold of Sachsen-Coburg elected King of the Belgians; separation of Belgium from the Netherlands.	V. Bellini, *Norma*. E. Delacroix, *La Liberté guidant le peuple*. V. Hugo, *Notre-Dame de Paris*.
1832	Demonstrations in Hambach urging democratic rule in Germany.	G. Donizetti, *L'Elisir d'Amore*. A. Pushkin, *Eugene Onegin*.

Testimonies

Thomas Carlyle

From the passionate longings and wailings of *Werther*, spoken as from the heart of all Europe; onwards through the wild unearthly melody of *Faust* (like the spirit-song of falling worlds); to that serenely smiling wisdom of *Meisters Lehrjahre*, and the German Hafiz, – what an interval; and all enfolded in an ethereal music, as from unknown spheres, harmoniously uniting all! A long interval; and wide as well as long: for this was a universal man. History, Science, Art, Human Activity under every aspect; the laws of light, in his *Farbenlehre*; the laws of wild Italian life in his *Benvenuto Cellini*; nothing escaped him, nothing that he did not look into, that he did not see into. Consider too the genuineness of whatsoever he did; his hearty, idiomatic way; simplicity with loftiness, and nobleness, and serial grace.

Death of Goethe. 1832

Herman Grimm

Almost too much has been said about Goethe already. There is a library of publications concerning him. Scarcely a week has passed recently that has not seen the appearance somewhere of a new piece by or about Goethe. And yet all this work on him offers only the beginnings of an investigation that must continue into the unforeseeable future.

Vorlesung über Goethe
[Lecture on Goethe]. *1874*

Emile Du Bois-Reymond

His theorising restricts itself to suggesting how from a primal phenomenon, as he calls it – which is, however, already a very complicated one – other phenomena arise, rather like one wisp of fog follows another, without an evident relationship. Goethe never understood the concept of mechanical causality. Hence his theory of colours, aside from its subjective part and in spite of his passionate efforts on its behalf during his long life, remained the stillborn bagatelle of an autodidactic dilettante.

Goethe und kein Ende
[Goethe and No End]. *1882*

Friedrich Nietzsche

Goethe belongs to a higher category of literature than what is represented by 'national literatures' . . . Only for a few did he really live and lives still: for most people he is nothing but a fanfare of vanity, that is trumpeted across the German border from time to time. Goethe, not merely a good and great man, but a culture – in the history of the Germans he is an interlude without consequences.

Menschliches, Allzumenschliches
[Human, All Too Human]. *1886*

Albert Schweitzer

Goethe was the first who experienced something akin to anxiety about humanity. In a time in which others were heedless, he was beginning to understand that the great problem in the coming stage of development would be how the individual could hold his own against the many.

Goethe-Gedenkrede
[Goethe-Memorial Lecture]. *1932*

Ernst Beutler

And today? The entire country lies in ruins, a creation a thousand years old, previously honoured by us as the repository of our history, as the dream and the realisation of the chain of our ancestors. The living despair. The dead accuse. Would it not be more fitting to observe this day in silence? Indeed, it would be, if it were the birthday of a statesman whose edifice lies in pieces. But this is the day of a poet. And the poet's country is one of words. Words and songs are eternal. Troy fell more than three thousand years ago, but Homer lives. And Goethe, too, lives and will continue to live and bear witness to the noblest and finest of which the German mind is capable; he will live as long as the Germans keep his memory, and thus themselves, alive. For that reason we should not keep silent on this day, but must speak.

> *Besinnung. Ansprache zur Feier von Goethes Geburtstag*
> [Contemplation. Address on the Occasion
> of Goethe's Birthday]. *1945*

Karl Jaspers

We should not idolize any human being. The era of the Goethe cult is past. To make possible a genuine succession we should not lose our awareness of the fragile foundations of humanity. Our real happiness about his greatness, the fact that we are deeply moved by the force of his love, should not prevent us from doing exactly what he himself tried to avoid: to behold the abyss. We experience relaxation and encouragement in Goethe's works, but not relief from the burden that has been laid upon us, not guidance through the world that is ours, which Goethe did not know. He is like a representative of humanity, but without offering us a path that we can follow. He is exemplary, without being a model.

> *Unsere Zukunft und Goethe*
> [Our Future and Goethe]. *1947*

Thomas Mann

The concepts of harmony, felicitous balance and classicism that we associate with Goethe's name were not simply a given, but a huge achievement, the work of forces of character that overcame daemonic-dangerous and possibly destructive tendencies, used, transformed and civilized them, diverted them to the good and useful. And yet there remains in this mighty existence much that is dark, superhuman-inhuman, which touches the simple humanitarian with cold and fear, thanks to the powerful dialectic of his nature, in which the divine and the diabolical, Faust's eternal striving and the mocking nihilism of Mephistopheles go separate poetic ways and contend with each other for truth.

Ansprache im Goethejahr 1949
[Address in the Goethe-Year 1949]

Robert M. Hutchins

For Goethe, men are united not merely by a common nature, but also by a common tradition. We are all links in the chain that connects the past with the future. The tradition transmits to us the aspirations and achievements of our ancestors and inspires us to struggle forward in our turn. The tradition is, therefore, a tradition of effort. This effort is directed to the realization of the maximum possibilities of mankind. It is a tradition of change; for Goethe hated violence. Change is to be produced by the conversion of men. Goethe is the great preacher of the moral, intellectual and spiritual revolution. Or, if revolution is too strong a word, though I think it is not, we can say with assurance that Goethe is the great apostle of incessant struggle to attain the highest aspirations of men through the fullest development of their highest powers.

Goethe and the Unity of Mankind. 1950

Hans Blumenberg

It is no exemplary life, that of this theatre director and collector of everything, not one of a possible guide and pointer toward discovering or inventing the meaning of existence. But, I ask on the other hand, is there any other life that we might have seen spread before us in such a multitude of relationships to reality and illusion? Whose development through self-understanding, loss of self, self-fiction, and self-disappointment would be similarly discernible for us?

Arbeit am Mythos
[Work on Myth]. *1979*

Ilse Graham

Goethe's all-comprehending goodness is sustained by the belief in an indestructible instinct upwards on the part of every living being, together with an utterly realistic complementary insight that baser possibilities lie dormant even in the finest and must be recognized in all their destructive dynamics, so that the redemption residing in the whole of creation can be achieved. This knowledgeable goodness would have stood the test even today, in spite of all the forces of evil around us, and that author's calmly incisive eye would not have been confused by what it saw. We have need of such as a guiding star in darkly chaotic times.

Goethe: Schauen und Glauben
[Goethe: Seeing and Believing]. *1988*

Nicholas Boyle

Goethe was the first poet who in virtue solely of his poetry, and not of its sublime or sacred subject-matter, or his contingent personal erudition, was also a secular sage. Indeed it would scarcely be too much to say that . . . Goethe created the very genre of lyric poetry as it is practised today: the book of shorter pieces linked not in the first instance formally or thematically, or by their devotional purpose or their suitability for musical setting, but by their origin in the discrete occasions of the poet's life, what he sees and reads and feels and thinks about, and all given meaning and importance not by any transcendent order but by their reference, explicit or implicit, to the poet's self and his activity of poetic making.

Goethe: The Poet and the Age. Volume 1:
The Poetry of Desire. 1991

Further Reading

All works listed are in English. The emphasis is on newer publications. More extensive bibliographies can be found in Williams' *Life of Goethe*, the Swales' *Reading Goethe*, and Sharpe's *Companion to Goethe*; they also cover works in German.

Translations

The Permanent Goethe. Edited, Selected and with an Introduction by Thomas Mann (New York: 1949): a one-volume compilation of excerpts from Goethe's literary works and his correspondence, reflecting Mann's personal preferences; various translators.

Goethe's Collected Works. Ed. Victor Lange, Eric Blackall and Cyrus Hamlin, 12 vols. (New York: 1983–1989; re-issue Princeton: 1994): translations of major works by Goethe, including some of his scientific studies; a collaborative effort of almost two dozen American and British authors.

Selected Works, introduced by Nicholas Boyle (New York: 2000): includes *Werther, Elective Affinities* and both parts of *Faust*, as well as a selection of poems; various translators.

Goethe, the Lyrist. 100 Poems. Transl. Edwin Zeydel (Chapel Hill: 1955): includes translations of an untitled poem and a stanza from the 'Epilogue to Schiller's Bell', quoted in this biography on pages 44-45 and 74 respectively.

Selected Poems. Ed. Christopher Middleton (London: 1983): includes translations of 'Blessed Longing', 'Testament' and 'O'er all the hill-tops', quoted in this biography on pages 88, 102–103 and 106 respectively.

Selected Poems. Transl. John Whaley (London: 1998): includes the translation of 'Elegy', quoted in this biography on page 97.

Selected Poetry. Transl. with an Introduction by David Luke (London: 2005): includes the translation of 'To the Moon', quoted in this biography on page 48.

Faust. Part One and Part Two. The Bayard Taylor translation, rev. and ed. by Stuart Atkins, 2 vols. (New York: 1962 and 1967): Taylor's translation, first published in 1871, has been reprinted many times. It reflects the original metre, although it may occasionally strike readers as old-fashioned (as does Goethe's language some German readers).

Faust. Part One and Part Two. Transl. with an Introduction by David Luke, 2 vols. (Oxford: 2008): an accurate and readable translation.

Faust: A Tragedy. Transl. Walter Arndt, ed. Cyrus Hamlin (New York: 2001): an elegant translation, augmented by interpretive notes and modern criticism.

Conversations of Goethe with Johann Peter Eckermann. Transl. John Oxenford, ed. J.K. Moorhead (New York: 1998): Eckermann's record of his conversations with Goethe is a rich source for Goethe's thought in his later years.

Letters from Goethe. Transl. M. von Herzfeld and C. Melvil Sym (Edinburgh: 1957): almost 600 letters from Goethe to a variety of recipients, ranging from his student years in Leipzig to the last days of his life.

Studies

Atkins, Stuart, *The Testament of Werther in Poetry and Drama* (Cambridge, MA: 1949): a study of the manifold responses to Werther in Germany and abroad.

Bennett, Benjamin, *Goethe's Theory of Poetry: 'Faust' and the Regeneration of Language* (Ithaca, NY: 1986): discusses the language and structural principles of Faust.

Blackall, Eric, *Goethe and the Novel* (Ithaca: 1976): interprets thematic and structural foundations of Goethe's narratives.

Boyd, James, *Goethe's Knowledge of English Literature* (New York: 1973): Goethe was an avid reader and admirer of English literature, from Shakespeare to Byron, Scott and Carlyle.

Boyle, Nicholas, *Goethe. The Poet and the Age*, 3 vols. (Oxford: 1991–): the most comprehensive biography of Goethe published in recent years; of three planned volumes, two (each with over 800 pages) have come out.

Bruford, Walter, *Culture and Society in Classical Weimar* (London: 1975): discusses social and cultural conditions in Weimar from Goethe's arrival there to the time of the Napoleonic wars.

Eissler, Kurt Robert, *Goethe: A Psychoanalytic Study* (Detroit: 1963): investigates the relations between Goethe and those close to him, particularly Charlotte von Stein.

Fairley, Barker, *A Study of Goethe* (Oxford: 1950): an attempt to explain the working of Goethe's mind. Fairley was one of the first scholars to reject the widespread cult of Goethe as an 'Olympian'.

Gray, Ronald, *Goethe the Alchemist* (Cambridge: 1952): discusses the significance of alchemical symbolism in Goethe's writings.

Leppmann, Wolfgang, *The German Image of Goethe* (Oxford: 1961): deals with the often tense relations between Goethe and his nation, as well as with the reception Germany afforded to him after his death.

Mason, Eudo, *Goethe's Faust. Its Genesis and Purport* (Berkeley: 1967): investigates scholarly criticism on Goethe's Faust relevant to the various stages of the play's history.

Reed, T.J., *The Classical Centre: Goethe and Weimar, 1775-1832* (London: 1986): discusses the concept of Weimar Classicism, represented primarily by Goethe and Schiller, as well as its significance for other writers, such as Hölderlin and Wieland.

Reiss, Hans, *Goethe's Novels* (London: 1969): a discussion of *Werther, Wilhelm Meister* and *Elective Affinities*.

Schulte, Hans, John K. Noyes, and Pia Kleber, *Goethe's Faust: Theatre of Modernity* (Cambridge: 2011): explores new aspects of *Faust*, with an illustrated section on the drama in modern performance.

Swales, Martin and Erika Swales, *Reading Goethe* (Rochester, NY: 2007): a critical introduction to the study of Goethe, with emphasis on his literary production.

Tantillo, Astrida Orle, *Goethe's Modernisms* (New York: 2010): discusses Goethe's influence on the development of Western society, as well as his criticism of modernity.

Wagner, Irmgard, *Critical Approaches to Goethe's Classical Dramas* (Columbia, SC: 1995): reviews scholarly studies of Goethe's dramas, particularly *Iphigenie* and *Tasso*.

Wellbery, David, *The Specular Moment: Goethe's Early Lyric and the Beginnings of Romanticism* (Stanford: 1996): interpretations of Goethe's poetry from the perspectives of semiotics and psychoanalytical rhetoric.

Wilkinson, Elizabeth and L.A. Willoughby, *Goethe, Poet and Thinker* (London: 1962): selected topics on Goethe's thought; a collaborative study by two of England's most respected scholars of German literature.

Williams, John R., *Goethe's Faust* (London: 1987): offers a broad tour d'horizon of the genesis and meaning of Goethe's Faust.

Williams, John R., *The Life of Goethe. A Critical Biography* (Oxford: 2001): a comprehensive study of Goethe's life and work, with chapters on his lyrical, dramatic, novelistic and scientific writings.

Collections, Periodicals

Bergstraesser, Arnold (ed.), *Goethe and the Modern Age* (Chicago: 1950): acta of the International Convocation held on the occasion of Goethe's 200th birthday, in Aspen, Colorado; includes contributions by Albert Schweitzer, Stephen Spender, Thornton Wilder and José Ortega y Gasset.

Brown, Jane, Meredith Lee and Thomas Saine (eds.), *Interpreting Goethe's Faust Today* (Columbia, SC: 1994): contemporary reflections on *Faust* by 23 American and European scholars.

Kuzniar, Alice (ed.), *Outing Goethe and His Age* (Stanford: 1996): 12 papers on gender and homosexuality relating to Goethe and some of his contemporaries.

Boyle, Nicholas and John Guthrie (eds.), *Goethe and the English-Speaking World* (Rochester, NY: 2002): 16 essays from a Cambridge symposium held to commemorate the 250th anniversary of Goethe's birth.

Sharpe, Lesley (ed.), *The Cambridge Companion to Goethe* (Cambridge: 2002): contemporary views of Goethe by British and American scholars, in 15 essays.

Bloom, Harold (ed.), *Johann Wolfgang von Goethe* (Philadelphia: 2003): 14 essays on Goethe's poetic works, reprinted from recently published journals and monographs.

Publications of the English Goethe-Society. New Series. (London: 1924–): presents papers read before the Society; published annually.

Goethe Yearbook (Columbia, SC: 1982–): articles and book reviews, published annually by the Goethe Society of North America.

Picture Sources

The author and publishers wish to express their thanks to the following sources of illustrative material and/or permission to reproduce it. They will make the proper acknowledgments in future editions in the event that any omissions have occurred.

Privately owned, Bloomington, Indiana: 104, 110
Stiftung Weimarer Klassik (Photos: Sigrid Geske, Weimar):
Goethe-Nationalmuseum: title page, 17, 20, 25 (Photo: Angelika Kittel), 35, 43, 46, 55, 57, 72, 77, 79, 84, 87, 90, 93, 95, 96, 100; Herzogin Anna Amalia Bibliothek: 8 (original of the manuscript: Stadt- und Universitätsbibliothek Frankfurt a. M.); Goethe-Schiller-Archiv: 27 (GSA 25/I, 2), 49 (GSA 29/468), 53 (GSA 27/9), 63 (GSA 26/LXI, 3, 16, Bl, 153), 70 (GSA 28/1046), 74 (GSA 25/XX, 9, I), 107 (GSA 25/XI, XV 15e)
Freies Deutsches Hochstift – Frankfurter Goethe-Museum, Frankfurt a. M. (Photos © Ursula Edelmann, Frankfurt a. M.): 5, 6, 57
Photo: Bildarchiv/ÖNB Wien: 10, 31, 69
© Bildarchiv Preußischer Kultur Besitz, Berlin, 1999: 15, 34
Goethe-Museum Düsseldorf (Photos: Walter Klein, Düsseldorf): 22, 38, 66, 81, 100, 117, 118
The correspondence between Duke Carl August and Goethe. Hans Wahl (ed.). Berlin 1915: 40
Parks of Weimar – Pictures by Günther Beyer. Weimar 1958: 42
Art Collections of Weimar (Photo: Eberhard Renno, Weimar): 47

Index